DALE EARNHARDT JR.

STANDING TALL IN THE SHADOW OF A LEGEND

LARRY COTHREN

FOREWORD BY
BENNY PHILLIPS

MOTORBOOKS
INTERNATIONAL

This edition first published in 2003 by Motorbooks International, an imprint of MBI Publishing Company, Galtier Plaza, Suite 200, 380 Jackson Street, St. Paul, MN 55101-3885 USA

Motorbooks International titles are also available at discounts in bulk quantity for industrial or sales-promotional use. For details write to Special Sales Manager at Motorbooks International Wholesalers & Distributors, Galtier Plaza, Suite 200, 380 Jackson Street, St. Paul, MN 55101-3885 USA.

Library of Congress Cataloging-in-Publication Data

Dale Eanrhardt, Jr. / by Primedia, Nigel Kinrade.
    p. cm.
  ISBN 0-7603-1517-5 (pbk. : alk. paper)
    1. Earnhardt, Dale, Jr. 2. Stock car drivers—United States—Biography. 3. Stock car racing—United States. I. Kinrade, Nigel. II Primedia Specialty Group.

GV1032.E19D36 2003
796.72'092—dc21
[B]

On the front cover: Few drivers in American auto racing command the marketplace appeal of Earnhardt Jr. *Doug Miller*

On the frontispiece: A company usually gets a lot of bang for its buck as one of Earnhardt Jr.'s sponsors. *Harold Hinson*

On the title page: A road course victory is one of the remaining milestones for Earnhardt Jr. *Nigel Kinrade*

On the back cover: Earnhardt Jr. celebrated in Charlotte's victory lane with Dad. *Harold Hinson*

Edited by Lee Klancher and Glen Grissom • Designed by Katie Sonmor • Layout by LeAnn Kuhlmann

Printed in China

CONTENTS

FOREWORD

BY BENNY PHILLIPS

On a May night that should have come rushing in like Christmas morning, Dale Earnhardt was madder than a pit bull at a poodle show. Dale Earnhardt Jr. had just captured the pole position for the Coca-Cola 600 at Lowe's Motor Speedway. The media rushed to the seven-time Winston Cup champion's truck to get "proud pop's" reaction.

Quicker than a jack-in-the-box, it was easy to see that Earnhardt Sr. was in a sullen mood. "Why don't you go ask him about the pole?" he said, "Hell, I wasn't driving the car, he was."

So members of the press made their way to see the kid who had just pulled off another major surprise. Grinning (and trying not to) like a possum eating persimmons, the kid explained how he drove the track—high into this turn, low into the next, and keeping a tight line all the way. He charmed the press like a grizzled old veteran.

The year was 2000 and "Little E" was a rookie on the Winston Cup circuit. He rocked the racing world with victories at Texas and Richmond, then booted experienced drivers aside and won The Winston at Charlotte during May.

He capped that impressive run by winning the pole for the 600 at Charlotte. What father would not be glowing like a Halloween lantern? Dale Earnhardt Sr., that's who.

"Why are you so ill?" I asked him the next day as he stood behind his rig.

"Who said I was ill," he snapped.

"Are you saying you were not ill last night?" I asked.

He smiled that little sly smile.

"Are you not proud of your own son?"

"You know I am," he replied, "and maybe I'm expecting too much from him. I wasn't mad about what happened last night. I guess I was still upset about what happened a couple of nights ago.

"It was after midnight, and I went over to his house and broke up this party. There were a bunch of his friends there. Listen, he can have parties. I like parties, but there is a time for everything, and I am so concerned about him being totally focused on racing. He should have his mind on the race this week instead of throwing a party. I think my greatest fear is that he will not be totally focused on racing.

"My son is not going to run a boot barn one week, operate a car dealership the next, play a guitar in between time, and ride a motorcycle around the country in his spare time. No! He's not going to do that and expect me to help support his racing efforts.

"I want him totally focused on racing. I'll be happy with that."

THE BEGINNING

BY LARRY COTHREN

From Cut-Out Cars to Myrtle Beach

The first race car Dale Earnhardt Jr. remembers putting his hands on was made of paper. He was just a toddler at the time, and he had only a vague notion of his father who was struggling to make it as a stock car racer.

"I didn't have any Matchbox cars, so I cut pictures of cars out of magazines and raced them at a table, as you would Matchbox cars," recalls Earnhardt Jr. His parents were divorced by the mid-1970s and the young tabletop racer was living with his mother.

"I knew a little bit about my father, but not a whole lot," he says. "I had never watched racing or known about racing at that time. I think I was interested in it at a very early age, even given the circumstances. Then once I did go live with my father, it just became more of an obsession. There was nothing like being eight, nine years old and playing with Matchbox cars in the living room while listening to Barney Hall talk about the race on the radio. It was just a great time, and it was fun. That escalated into going to the races as I got older."

Even then, Earnhardt Jr. had a sense of his rightful place in the sport.

"I wasn't really into working on the cars or knowing or learning about the cars," he says. "I was just really interested in what it was like being a driver and the things you had to do. I started watching my dad more, as far as watching him drive and trying to figure out why he did this or why he did that, or why the

By age 18, Earnhardt Jr. had become a full-time racer. *Harold Hinson*

Dad hangs on to "Little E" at Charlotte Motor Speedway in the mid-1970s. Others pictured are Dale Sr.'s brothers, Randy (middle) and Danny, and Danny's wife Sherry.
Gary Hargett Collection

car wasn't working and what he was doing to fix it and how they fixed it.

"Then when I turned 13, I remember sitting there one night in the living room with my dad and I wanted so badly to race, but I knew it was three more years before I even got a driver's license. I just could not comprehend having to wait three more years. I was about to go crazy. You know what I mean? That's how bad I really wanted it at that point. I told Daddy, 'I've got to do something because I can't wait for three more years.' It was just too long. I had never wanted something or craved anything as bad ever before. He just told me, 'Man, you've got to be patient.' I don't think he took me quite as seriously as I was at that time."

No Mercy

The skinny teenager who showed up at Andy Hillenburg's driving school in 1992 was much like hundreds of others who have graduated from the program. Young racers chasing a dream and looking for an advantage come through Hillenburg's school week after week, month after month, year after year.

Earnhardt Jr. is shown with his late-model Chevrolet at North Wilkesboro Speedway in 1993. *Harold Hinson*

This kid was different though. The shy youngster with the slight build showed up as the son of the greatest stock car racer ever. He was the third generation in a line of stock car thoroughbreds who epitomized hard-core, stand-on-the-gas driving. From the very moment Dale Earnhardt Jr. decided to become a racer, he was sure to have that fact hovering over him. That was true when he showed up at Hillenburg's driving school as a 17-year-old wannabe, just a month away from his 18th birthday, and it would be true for the rest of his life. Being a stock-car-driving Earnhardt would mean more than being just another kid in a driving school.

Dale Earnhardt Jr., then just a wisp of a teenage boy, quickly lived up to the Earnhardt name during that week at Hillenburg's school in September of 1992. When the engine exploded in one of Hillenburg's cars with Earnhardt Jr. behind the wheel, it blew a connecting rod clean out of the block. Granted, the car did have an experimental engine because Hillenburg's mechanics were searching for the right engine combination to use in the school's cars. But Hillenburg says, "He didn't show it any mercy."

Yes, this kid was an Earnhardt.

"You could tell even then that he was determined to try to make it work," says Hillenburg, "and you could tell that if he didn't have the experience, he was going to get it and if he didn't have the talent, he was going to figure it out and get the talent. There was a lot of determination on his part."

Hard driving and determination are dominant traits in the Earnhardt gene pool. Ralph Earnhardt, Dale's father, was a terror on dirt tracks around the Carolinas in the 1950s until his 1973 death from a heart attack at age 45. Long before Dale became The Intimidator, Ralph was tearing

it up on short tracks, and he became the standard by which Saturday-night racers all around were measured. That was true at Concord, Charlotte, Hickory, Columbia, Gaffney, Asheville, Greenville, Spartanburg, Lancaster, Monroe, and every other short track around the two Carolinas. "Anywhere he went, when he pulled in you knew he was the man to beat," recalls Ned Jarrett, who competed against Ralph in NASCAR's Sportsman division, primarily in the 1950s when both men won national titles.

When Dale began eyeing a career as a stock car driver in the late 1960s and early 1970s, he had to make his own way. He learned what he could from Ralph, but Dale built his own cars and put together his own deals to drive the cars of others. Ralph made sure that Dale learned the trade on his own, and that became the Earnhardt way.

Twenty years later when Junior began embarking on a driving career, he was expected to work on his own cars and learn lessons the hard way. "I don't know that Dale ever really sat down and actually told Junior how to drive a race car," says Gary Hargett, who owned the late-model Chevrolets that Earnhardt Jr. drove in the mid-1990s. "He never did. He never would

At age 17, Earnhardt Jr. attended Andy Hillenburg's driving school at Charlotte Motor Speedway. *Stock Car Racing Archives*

go to the race track with him, and I think a lot of that came from the way Ralph was. Dale wanted Junior to know if he was going to learn, he was going to learn it on his own."

So while Earnhardt Jr. no doubt enjoyed advantages that other young drivers could only dream about, he was essentially left to his own devices. That, and the pure grit he soon displayed, helped Earnhardt Jr. earn respect from his fellow competitors, such as those he raced against at Myrtle Beach (South Carolina) Speedway, where he and Hargett raced regularly in the late-model division.

There were, nonetheless, some hard lessons to be learned. Hard-core racers populate Myrtle Beach Speedway on a Saturday night. Some are racing just as a hobby, but many hope to be the next Dale Earnhardt, Rusty Wallace, or Jeff Gordon. These are guys who would take out *anybody* for a shot at victory lane. If they happened to take out Dale Earnhardt's kid, then all the better. Plus, it was hard for Junior to shake the "rich kid gone racing" perception that many of the competitors had of him at the fast little half-mile track. It all combined to make Myrtle Beach Speedway a tough place to send an 18-year-old to learn the ropes.

Hargett, a short-track veteran now in his fifth decade as a car owner, teamed with Junior for a few races in 1992, the year Junior turned 18 years old. Then Hargett and Junior ran the full late-model schedule at Myrtle Beach Speedway for three consecutive seasons from 1993 to 1995.

"The first year we ran down there everybody wanted to turn Junior around," says Hargett. "I mean, it would be every week. I told him he was just going to have to take it because they were all going to do it. I said, 'Everybody who races wants to run over Dale Earnhardt. Well, they're never going to get the chance to run over your daddy, so they're going to take it out on you.' And they roughed him up bad that first year."

Before the last race that season, Hargett put the word out that he would no longer tolerate other drivers running into Earnhardt Jr.

"I kept Junior off of you all year," Hargett said at the drivers' meeting. "You've had your fun, you've run over an Earnhardt all year long, and it's over with now. For the next man that hits him, I'm going to let him hit you back. You'll just keep doing it if you want to."

The message didn't sink in until late in the race when Earnhardt Jr. was on his way to winning.

"There was a boy down there from Monck's Corner [a small town in South Carolina] who turned Junior on the last lap, and we were leading the race," says Hargett. "He spun him out, and I told Junior, 'The next race you run, you need to get him right quick. If you don't, they're going to keep doing this to you as long as you race.'

"We went back to a big race they have down there, a special event in November, and I had really forgotten about it. But we started, I don't know, 9th, 10th, 11th, somewhere along there, and this boy was on the inside of the row right in front of Dale Jr. Well, they gave the green, and when they went down into turn one, Junior just turned him the wrong way and he went through a steel gate down there. Before they got to the backstretch, Junior said, 'Well, was that good enough?' I

Although just a teenager, Earnhardt Jr.'s driving style proved to be true to the family name at Andy Hillenburg's driving school. *Stock Car Racing Archives*

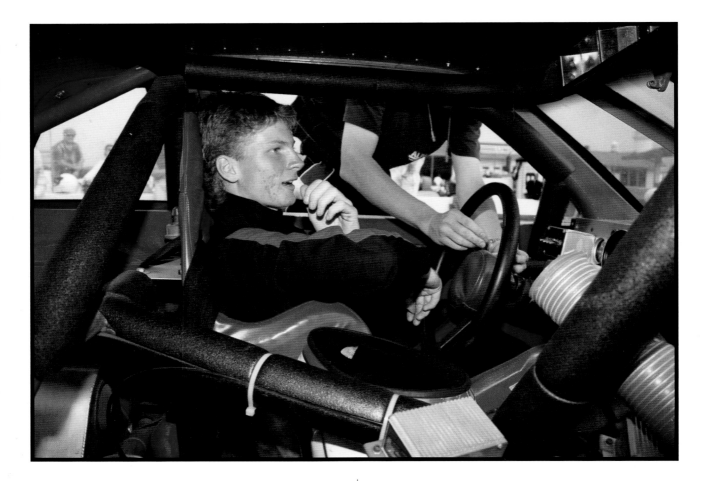

The cockpit of a race car would become a familiar place.
Stock Car Racing Archives

said, 'Yeah, if you didn't kill him, it is.'

"Every week, they would beat on that back bumper, beat on that back bumper. But I don't know of anybody else who every really turned him after that."

It wasn't the first time Junior had taken the initiative. Earlier that season, a squabble with another driver ended on pit road as Junior confronted the guy before the start of a race, leaving Hargett with one of his favorite stories. "Dale Jr. stopped him," recalls Hargett, "and told him, 'Look, we can solve this problem we've got now. I'll put my race car out on the race track and you bring yours out there. We'll take off and you go that way and I'll go this way and we'll run head-on on the backstretch. The boy said, 'You're crazy.' And Junior told him, 'That's exactly right—I'm crazy.' And they never had any more problems."

"Well, talk to the man."

To get to Gary Hargett's garage, drive about an hour southeast of Charlotte and its deeply rooted stock car culture, where most of NASCAR's top teams are located. Go through Marshville, North Carolina, home place of country music star Randy Travis, and turn off of Highway 74 to cover the last eight miles on a two-lane road that stretches across gently rolling North Carolina farmland. Go a mile or so past Hargett's Store at the crossroads and turn right onto a gravel driveway beside the wooden roadside sign etched with the words "Gary Hargett Racing." The simplicity of the surrounding countryside and the small garage sitting beside the short gravel road is deceiving, for there's nothing simple or nondescript about Gary Hargett's 40-plus years of

Earnhardt Jr. raced three full seasons at Myrtle Beach Speedway in the mid-1990s. *Gary Hargett Collection*

making a living as a racer.

Hargett teamed with driver Harry Gant in the early 1970s and won Sportsman (now NASCAR Busch Series) races all over the country. Gant and Hargett won 38 of 43 races at one point in the mid-1970s, before Gant moved on to a successful career in NASCAR Winston Cup. Hargett later fielded a Sportsman car for Dale Earnhardt Sr. and won with him. When he was getting his start in the 1950s and 1960s, Hargett rubbed elbows with the likes of NASCAR legends Ralph Earnhardt, Curtis Turner, Speedy Thompson, and Jack Ingram.

Hargett's small office, tucked inside a corner of the garage, is filled with racing photos and memorabilia collected during his five decades in the sport. There's a framed picture of Ralph Earnhardt sitting on the back of his Camaro sometime around 1970. Another picture shows Dale, shirttail hanging out of his jeans, standing outside Hargett's garage beside a Camaro he and Hargett campaigned when they first started racing together in the mid-1970s.

Hargett was tight with the Earnhardts. He bought a new race car from Ralph in the early 1960s and Ralph even occasionally raced the car for Hargett. Later, Dale and Hargett formed a

Earnhardt Jr.'s sister, Kelley, looked on during an interview at Myrtle Beach Speedway. *Gary Hargett Collection*

The number 3 late-model Chevrolet gets serviced at a short track near Greenville, North Carolina. *Gary Hargett Collection*

Junior accepts an award for finishing fourth in late-model stocks at Myrtle Beach Speedway in 1995.
Gary Hargett Collection

friendship, raced together, and then kept in touch while Dale was becoming a stock car icon in the 1980s. During that time, Hargett was working on a Winston Cup car for Mike Potter and he and Dale occasionally talked at the race track. Hargett is quick to point out that the relationship was hot and cold; it was built upon and held back by the tempestuous nature of both men.

Although out of Winston Cup by the late 1980s, Hargett continued to race local tracks and field cars for whoever was willing to pay the bills. In the 1990s, Hargett began crossing paths again with Dale Earnhardt. Gary Hargett and the Earnhardts began an association that lasted until Earnhardt Jr. moved on to run his own late-model deal for a season or two, and then moved full-time to the Busch Series.

It was 1991 when Hargett, while fielding a car for an aspiring teenage driver at Concord (North Carolina) Motorsport Park, first took notice of Earnhardt's kid.

"Dale Junior came out to Concord and had a little street stock he ran with [his half brother] Kerry," recalls Hargett. "They would swap back and forth. I was at the race track one day and I told Dale, 'How about letting me put Junior in a late-model car?' He said, 'Ahhh, you don't want to fool

Earnhardt Jr. in action at Myrtle Beach Speedway.
Kevin Thorne

with him.' That was just the way Dale was. Every week I would ask him again and we would talk about it.

"The funniest thing is he asked me one day, 'You know which one you're talking about now?' Because at that age, Kerry looked just like Dale Sr., and Dale Jr. looked like his mother. He didn't look like an Earnhardt. Junior looked like he took from his mother and [her father] Robert Gee's side of the family. He had almost blonde hair, and he was a little bitty fellow. Kerry was tall, had dark hair, and a moustache. Dale asked me, 'You sure you know which one you're talking about now?' I said, 'Yeah, I know exactly which one I want.' Junior was just as wild as wild could be, and he would run wide open all the way around the race track in that street stock, just smoking the tires.

"Well, Dale finally broke down. I think what really did it was we were over at Charlotte practicing and I told Dale about it again. He said, 'Man, I don't want to fool with that. You don't want to do that.' Well, I got mad and just turned around and walked off. I was going down through the parking lot and some man hollered at me. I turned around and it was [Richard] Childress [who owned Dale Sr.'s number 3 Chevrolet]. Richard came up there and said, 'You not getting anywhere with him.' I said, 'No, that man is not going to spend any money.' He said, 'Well, if he won't help you then let me know. I'll help you out. We'll put him in a car.'

"Anyway, a day or two after that, Dale called me. I knew they had talked. Dale told me to come over to his shop and talk about this thing. I went over there to Mooresville—where they're at now, but they just had that one old shop then—and I went in and he said, 'You still want to do that deal?' And I said, 'Yeah.' Dale said, 'Well, let's go out here and talk to him.'

"Junior was out there sanding on a car in a paint booth. He was a little bitty fellow. He didn't look like he was 12 years old, but I guess he was 16 or 17 at the time. Dale Jr., I really believe, was always afraid of Dale Sr. He wouldn't say a word around him. He wouldn't even look at him eye to eye. It was like he was always scared to death. We went back to where Dale Jr. was working and Dale said, 'Junior! Do you want to drive this man's race car?' Junior just glanced up and said, 'Yeah, yeah,' and kept on working. He wouldn't even look at me. Dale said, 'Well, talk to the man then if you want to drive his race car!'

"Dale left and Junior was just like a little kid then. He was ready to go racing. So we worked out a deal. I had a car I had built for the other boy who was driving. It was a true late-model stock. We worked out a deal where Dale [Sr.] paid for the motors and the tires, and we just went out, put him in it, went to Myrtle Beach, and went at it."

The goals were simple, according to those associated with the late-model effort. Ernie Hammonds became acquainted with Earnhardt Jr. and Hargett soon after they began racing at Myrtle Beach. The three formed a bond, with Hammonds eventually serving as parts courier during the week, chauffeur for Junior on weekends, and crewman on race day. "When I would go to Mooresville, to DEI," recalls Hammonds, "and pick up the oil and whatever parts we needed for the race car, Dale would say, 'Seat time and laps is all I'm interested in. Then when we get to the Busch Series, we'll worry about winning races.' And evidently he knew exactly what he was talking about."

Car owner Gary Hargett (far left) joined Earnhardt Jr. for a personal appearance at Myrtle Beach, one of the first such appearances by Little E. *Gary Hargett Collection*

Rednecks from Mooresville

BY LARRY COTHREN

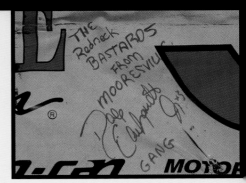

Sheet metal hanging in Gary Hargett's garage commemorates a late-model race at Hickory, North Carolina. *Larry Cothren*

Although most of Dale Earnhardt Jr.'s early short-track experience came at Myrtle Beach Speedway, it wasn't the only track where he and car owner Gary Hargett raced in the mid-1990s.

While they were well accepted at most places, they sometimes visited tracks where the locals were less than thrilled to see an Earnhardt. That was the case on their first trip to a short track near Greenville, North Carolina, where the owner offered appearance money for them to show up and race.

"That was Rusty Wallace country," says Hargett. "When I got there I found that out right quick. We go out there and earn the pole, set a new track record the first time we went. In the race, a guy blocked us in on pit road and wouldn't let us out, so we lost a lap. We came back out, got our lap back, and finished second or third maybe, but we had to fight our way out of the race track.

"I was up on top of the trailer and those people wouldn't let me down. Junior drove the car up in the trailer and we shut the door and left him in there, got in the truck, and drove out of the race track. We got out on the road and the man came out there and gave us our money and asked us if we would come back the next week. I said, 'No, I don't think so.' But we went back three or four times and always ran good there. Those people did not like Earnhardts in that part of the country, but that promoter loved it."

Once at a race at Hickory (North Carolina) Motor Speedway, the crowd—and Earnhardt Jr.'s crew—became unruly because of an incident during the race.

"We were like 3rd or 4th fastest in practice but we were 35th or something in qualifying," recalls Hargett. "So they came up with a track provisional to put Junior in the race. Anyway, we started last, and we were running over everybody on the race track and got to third or fourth. Then they had a red flag for a funeral, which they do at Hickory. If they have a funeral over there, they stop the race because the cemetery is right beside the race track. So they stopped the race and we sat there for a long time.

"I noticed an official over talking to Junior and I asked what he wanted. Junior said, 'They're going to send us to the rear, said we jumped the restart on the last restart.' Well, we had run 50 laps since the last restart. So why didn't they black-flag us then? Later I found out what the deal was. He had run over one of the Setzers (a popular racing family in the Hickory area), and after the red flag they decided they were going to put us in the rear.

"Well, there wasn't but 10 laps or less to run, so I told Junior to park the car. He pulled out and came around and stopped right in the middle of pit road. Those people in the stands went berserk. They were throwing bottles, rocks, and sticks, because they hated Earnhardts in Hickory, too. We were throwing stuff at the grandstand, and they were throwing stuff at us. Somebody had torn a fender off, so one of the guys on the crew grabbed the fender and ran out there and threw it toward the grandstands.

"There was some guy in the stands who stood up, and I could hear him holler just as good, and he said: 'Yeah, you redneck bastards from Mooresville, go on back home.'"

The incident is commemorated on the wall of Hargett's garage, where a piece of sheet metal from one of the cars he and Earnhardt Jr. campaigned now hangs high on the wall. The sheet metal has an inscription from Earnhardt Jr.: "The redneck bastards from Mooresville, Dale Earnhardt Jr.'s gang."

Myrtle Beach Speedway lies 150 miles south of Gary Hargett's garage in Marshville. Although there are dozens of short tracks in the Charlotte area, many within an hour's drive of Marshville, Dale Earnhardt chose Myrtle Beach Speedway as the place to officially begin Junior's career. It was a stroke of genius.

At the tracks closer to Charlotte—those in Hickory or Concord, for example—Junior was sure to be under an intense microscope, both from the public and from the media. After all, this was the son of stock car racing's biggest star and his every move would be scrutinized. Junior's older sister Kelley and half-brother Kerry were getting started in late-models at the same time, but at different tracks. Dale thought it was important for the three of them to race separately, each making his or her own way. At Myrtle Beach, under the tutelage of Hargett, Junior could focus on racing against some of the best short-track racers to be found anywhere.

"To me, that's the perfect race track for somebody to start out at," says Hargett. "They call it a half-mile, but it's a big race track, and it's got long corners. They're not real tight corners, and the race track is wide. If you get into trouble, you've got room to get yourself out of it, and you get used to running real fast down the straightaways, so it's an easy race track to learn on. Now, if you hit the wall, you tear up stuff because you're running so fast. But 10 cars can spin out on the straightaway and

Gary Hargett raced with all three Earnhardts—Ralph, Dale, and Dale Jr. *Larry Cothren*

you've still got room where you can get around them without getting in a lot of trouble. You get used to the car getting out of shape a little bit, but you've got enough room to get it gathered back up too."

Yet, the potential that Hargett saw during Earnhardt Jr.'s street stock days at Concord needed some refinement. The natural ability—the feel for a race car, the willingness to mash the throttle, the on-track timing, all of it—was there. Raw but unrefined talent had been his daddy's trademark back in the 1970s, and it was the same with Earnhardt Jr. running Myrtle Beach and stepping up from street stocks to late-models.

"He ran good right off," says Hargett. "Like I said, he was the wildest thing you've ever seen on the race track. He would run sideways all the way around that track. I could not get it out of him, but I remembered Dale was the same way. He would run over people. If they were in the way, he would run over them. I remember Neil Bonnett was talking about that one time and said about Dale, 'That's the roughest boy I've ever seen in my life.' That was when he first started, and Junior was about the same way, though, for a while.

"But he was smart, although he would argue with you about what the car was doing. I mean, from day one, he would tell you exactly what he wanted that car to do. We didn't agree on it a whole lot, but I would try it just to show him that he was wrong. But he wasn't always wrong. He had a feel for a race car, and if I told him he could run wide open all the way around that race track, he would try it. And if I told him he had to get on the brakes at this point or this point, he would do that, too. He would do exactly what I told him to do.

"Still, when the race started, he was going to run pretty much the way he wanted to run. One thing that really impressed me right off the bat, and I didn't tell him and I know his daddy never told him, is that if that race car quit working somewhere on that race track—say he's chopping the bottom off and was real fast but it quit working down there—then he would find somewhere else on that race track that he could go and make that car run. He did that from the first year he ever raced, and he still does it now. If he told you he thought it was too stiff in the front or too soft in the front, most of the time he was right. He had a natural feel for what the race car was doing."

"He was a good race car driver," says Ernie Hammonds. "The first year Gary had to coach him through everything. He had the natural talent, but he was just so eager to go to the front that if you were in his way, you were going to move. Little by little, he got better at it. About halfway through the second year, he was a whole lot like, well, he reminded me of Rusty Wallace. He drove a lot more like Rusty than Dale Earnhardt."

The biggest obstacle for a young racer to overcome at Myrtle Beach Speedway is the intense competition. The Powell brothers—Robert, Charles, and half-brother Sean Graham—have ruled the roost at Myrtle Beach Speedway for a decade or so, and few have challenged their supremacy. Junior won just once in his three seasons there. The often-told story is that when Dale Sr. heard about the win, his first question was, "Did you beat the Powell brothers? Because if they weren't there, you didn't win anything."

For the record, the Powells weren't there on August 20, 1994, when Junior won his first late-model feature at Myrtle Beach Speedway. Ditto for his next win there, in 1996. "They gave Junior a hard time because he didn't win, but nobody wins on a regular basis and beats the Powell family at Myrtle Beach," says Hammonds. "Between the three, they've probably won 250 races at Myrtle Beach Speedway, or pretty close. Don't get me wrong, there are other people who've won here, but if you come here and you beat those three people, you've earned your money—no matter what your name is. They gave Junior a hard time because he couldn't, but it's not easy for anybody."

Robert Powell was nearing 30 when Earnhardt Jr. began racing at the beach. By the time Earnhardt Jr. came along, Powell had long been dominant on some of South Carolina's top short tracks, including Summerville, Columbia, Anderson, and Myrtle Beach. Powell was NASCAR Weekly Racing Series National Champion in 1988, the year he won 23 of 31 races at Summerville, and he later began winning regularly at Myrtle Beach.

"Junior gave Robert a whole lot of credit for his learning to drive a race car because he finished behind him probably seven or eight races a year—right behind him," recalls Hammonds. "We could get close enough to get second—or fourth or fifth behind the three of them—but we couldn't get by them. They were the three who beat him on a regular basis. It was still a lot of fun."

Powell says they had even more fun during Friday- night shows at another area track.

"We had our best times racing at a little short track in Florence," says Powell. "It's a flat, worn-out, drivers' race track. He was good over there. You know, he was wild as heck anyway. We would run into each other and, I mean, we had fun. He told me one year, 'You know why I always run into you on the race track? You remind me so much of my daddy it makes me sick.'

"I knew he was going to be good, though. He wasn't scared of nothing. Wide open. He always handled himself good, too. He's probably one of the few racers I never really had a problem with. He's like me. You come here to race and you race. Rubbing is racing. That's the way I race, and people who can't handle that get mad. The two of us, we would rub and beat and bang and then get out and laugh about it. Because we knew we wouldn't wreck each other, just race.

"I remember one time we got rough, and I kind of got mad at him. I said, 'Man, are you crazy?' He said, 'What are you talking about? We were just having fun.' He ran into the side of me, knocked me to the top of the race track, and passed me. I would go back by him and he would get

"I was just the general flunky . . . but I had a whole lot of fun, and I'll never forget it," says Ernie Hammonds of his days hanging out with Earnhardt Jr. at Myrtle Beach. *Larry Cothren*

The Earnhardts—Kelley, 16-year-old Dale Jr., Teresa, and Dale Sr.—at the 1990 Winston Cup awards banquet. *Stock Car Racing Archives*

into the side of me, knock me to the top of the race track, and go back by me. Finally, I just ran into him and knocked him about off the race track."

Despite the skirmishes, or because of them, the two developed a mutual respect. Earnhardt Jr. sometimes sought advice from his older competitor. "He would come to me a good bit," says Powell. "But Dale Jr. pretty much stayed to himself. We raced here together for three years. The first year I bet we didn't speak four or five words. I know how it is, or I felt I knew how it was with him. Everybody is always trying to ride him and all. I just took him as Dale Jr. That's the way I am. I think he took me the same way. He knew I didn't look at him as a rich kid or whatever, because I knew he struggled and he had to earn what he got.

"I never saw him where it was like he had to do this. You know what I'm saying? He would just take it as it comes. It's almost like, looking back now, he knew where he was going and he knew what he had to do to get where he was going. No matter how he did it, he was going to be there. Like I tell everybody, you've still got to be able to do it. I don't care how much money you've got, you've still got to be able to drive. And he could drive a race car."

"You were not going to beat him."

The speedway is a small part of the fabric of life in Myrtle Beach, which is one of the most popular vacation spots on the East Coast. The area is rich with tourist attractions—or distractions if you're young, single, and away from home for one of the first times in your life. Earnhardt Jr. and company came to race, but they were also intent on enjoying themselves.

Through the week, Earnhardt Jr. often stayed with the Hargetts, stretching out in a sleeping bag at their home near the race shop. He and Gary would prepare the car during the day, with Earnhardt Jr. showing an aptitude for chassis setups and decisions on changing shocks and springs on the car. Then on Saturday mornings, Hargett and Earnhardt Jr. would leave Hargett's garage and make the two-and-a-half-hour drive to Myrtle Beach. They would unload the car, turn laps during an early practice session, and hit the area attractions. That meant swimming on the beach or at a motel pool, playing video games, or riding go-carts. The group normally included Earnhardt Jr., Hargett, Ernie Hammonds, and one or two others who were helping with the car at that particular time.

Earnhardt Jr. and Hargett would occasionally spend time at a souvenir shop owned by Nick Lucas, part owner of Myrtle Beach Speedway. Earnhardt Jr. would sign autographs and hang out. Hammonds ran the souvenir shop for Lucas and it was there where he got to know Earnhardt Jr. and Hargett. "Junior would look through there and see if I had any new Darrell Waltrip stuff, because believe it or not Darrell Waltrip and Jimmy Means were his heroes, not daddy," recalls Hammonds. "That's pretty amazing. We would leave from there and go down on the beach and play those pole position games for hours and hours and hours, then ride up and down the beach.

"He would come back to the race track at about one o'clock and start doing his part of the deal. Sometimes he would wait until four or five, but by five o'clock he'd be there. We would stay there for the racing deal. Then when it was over, we would go to the beach and play the games, and go eat, then go on the beach and ride. He would spend a couple hours sometimes just riding up and down the beach, because he never had any freedom. I mean, this was the first freedom Dale Jr. had away from his daddy."

The autograph sessions at the Myrtle Beach souvenir shop were small, informal affairs compared to the ones Earnhardt Jr. encountered later on. "He was real shy, real, real shy," says Hammonds. "I went with him and did the first really big autograph session he did at the opening of a Wal-Mart in Charlotte—I think it was in 1993—where seven- or eight-hundred people showed up and fifty people came through there before he ever spoke. He would sign, but just hold his head down."

The shyness did little to mask a competitive streak and a level of determination that left an impression on both Hargett and Hammonds. It became obvious during the Myrtle Beach days that this was another Earnhardt who was going places in stock car racing.

"I didn't even put the Earnhardt into the deal," says Hammonds. "I knew as competitive as he was and as bad as he wanted to race that he would make it. Every time I went anywhere with him, we would get in a go-cart or play a video game with a race car on it—that's how I knew he was going to make it. That's all he wanted to do. And you were not going to beat him. You were *not*

It was clear early on that Earnhardt Jr. would have a lot to live up to. *Jerry Haislip*

going to beat him. We would go to the go-cart track and he was going to beat you, no matter who you were or when it was. And you couldn't beat him on the video games, and still can't."

The go-cart races often turned into slam-bang affairs, with Earnhardt Jr. giving no quarter.

"As a matter of fact, Junior put me in the hospital down there one Saturday afternoon," says Hargett, laughing at the memory. "He turned me over in the go-cart and broke my ribs. They had to carry me to the hospital and get me taped up. What happened was we were beating and banging and he spun me out, then drove up over the wheel and into my side with his front bumper. Then he got out laughing about it."

Occasionally, the nightlife around Myrtle Beach left its mark on Junior.

"I guess my favorite story is from when we had a big late-model race here one November," says Hammonds. "We had been out and had quite a few drinks the night before. Junior stopped on the track and said, 'I've got to have something to drink,' while the race was under caution. Gary told him, 'We can't bring you anything to drink out there.' He said, 'Get Ernie to bring me some water.' So I take him a cup of water out there.

"Kelley, his sister, is out there and she's hollering at me, 'Don't take him any water. He needs to learn better.' So I take him that cup anyway. Then he hollers back on the radio, 'Bring me some more.' So I take him some more. So then he hollers, 'I've got to have another drink.'

"Benny Parsons and his son Kevin were at the race. Kevin tried racing here for a little while and was here for that race. Junior said, 'Go by Benny's trailer and get me a Coke.' So I went over and said, 'Benny, Junior wants to know if you've got a Coke he can have?' He said, 'How are you going to get it out there?' I said I would take it to him. He said, 'I wonder what his daddy would think if I told him this story?' I said 'Please don't do that, Benny.'

"Luckily I was good enough friends with people at the race track where I could walk out and take him a drink—or I don't know what might have happened. They asked what I was doing out there and I said my buddy is going to die if I don't get him something to drink."

For the most part, the people who had close contact with Earnhardt Jr. during the Myrtle Beach days have little contact with him today, although Hammonds still talks to him on the telephone and sees him occasionally. The weekly phone calls Earnhardt Jr. used to make to Hargett when Earnhardt Jr. first started running the Busch Series have stopped, and the two haven't talked in the two years since Earnhardt Sr.'s death. "A month after Dale Sr. got killed, Junior was like a different person altogether," says Hargett.

Robert Powell, the short-track ace, saw Earnhardt Jr. in Darlington soon after Earnhardt Jr. moved to the Busch Series. Earnhardt Jr. called out to him as Powell walked by and the two spent a few minutes together. They've talked very little since then.

Hammonds relishes the time he spent with Hargett and Earnhardt Jr. and is modest about his role in Earnhardt Jr.'s Myrtle Beach experience. "I was just the general flunky," says Hammonds. "I was the general flunky who tried to get Junior where he needed to be at the right time, but it was fun. It was really neat. I mean, I can say I hauled Earnhardt's kid around, and up and down the road. I wouldn't trade it for anything I've ever done in my life. I didn't make any money, but I had a whole lot of fun and I'll never forget it."

MOVING UP

BY LARRY COTHREN

From Myrtle Beach to the Busch Series

All eyes were on Dale Earnhardt Jr. Everyone wanted to know if he would follow in his father's championship footsteps. *Paul Melhado*

By 1996, Dale Earnhardt Jr. and team owner Gary Hargett had parted ways. The two won just one race together, at Myrtle Beach in 1994, before going winless in 1995. Hargett's Marshville shop served as the center of his and Earnhardt Jr.'s racing activity for three seasons, but Earnhardt Sr. wanted the team to be headquartered in Mooresville for the 1996 season. Hargett turned down Earnhardt Sr.'s offer of a job in the Mooresville shop. After years of being his own boss, Hargett felt he couldn't take orders from someone else, particularly Earnhardt Sr.—someone Hargett knew to be every bit as headstrong as Hargett himself.

So, during the 1996 and 1997 seasons, Earnhardt Jr. drove a car built in his father's shop in Mooresville. The shop was small in comparison to the mega-shops prevalent today, but it was the forerunner to the complex that now houses Dale Earnhardt, Inc. Earnhardt Sr., just beginning to really make his mark as a team owner, was fielding a competitive Craftsman Truck Series team and a fledgling Busch Series team out of the Mooresville shop. Ron Hornaday had won six times and finished third in points while driving Earnhardt's truck during the inaugural truck series season in 1995. Hornaday then won four races and claimed the series title the next season. By 1997, with Steve Park as a rookie driver, Earnhardt's Busch Series team was ready for another full season. Earnhardt Jr.'s late-model cars were built in 1996 and 1997 by some of the same crewmen who built the trucks and the Busch cars, with Earnhardt Jr. providing assistance.

Earnhardt Jr. competed at several different tracks—Myrtle Beach, Nashville, and I-95 Speedway in Florence (South Carolina), among them—during the two seasons his late-model cars were built in Mooresville. The results were not significantly different from what he experienced in Hargett's car; the effort was still just a step away from consistently visiting victory lane.

"We ran 16 races at I-95 [Florence] in 1996," recalls Earnhardt Jr. "I finished second 14 times. We won one race and the engine blew up in the other race. We were mainly just bouncing around, from Nashville to Florence to Myrtle Beach."

He added a win at Myrtle Beach to the one at Florence in 1996 before going winless again the next season. The Busch Series was beckoning Earnhardt Jr. by then, however, as he started his first Busch race at Myrtle Beach Speedway on June 22, 1996. He then ran eight Busch races in 1997. His record in those events was nothing spectacular, with only one top ten, a seventh place at Michigan on August 16, 1997. There was certainly no hint of the Busch success that would follow over the next two years.

By the end of 1997, his late-model career was over, although Earnhardt Jr. can still recite his record in NASCAR's Weekly Racing Series: 159 starts and 3 wins.

"It was a good time," he says. "I learned an awful lot about driving and quite a bit about race cars. That's really the only time in my career where I worked on my own equipment, and for the most part did probably 80 percent of the job on my car, getting the car down to the track and driving it. Doing those things was fun. It was great because you were on your own schedule pretty much and you knew what you had to do to get the car ready for the next race.

"You don't really find Winston Cup or Busch Series drivers these days coming from the late-model ranks as often as you used to. You used to get a lot of late-model drivers out of the Winston Racing Series into the Busch Series, but you don't anymore. I think it's overlooked now because it's not a highly publicized series like it used to be. I wouldn't trade the four years I raced the Winston Racing Series for anything because I think it was a great, great foundation for the driver I became in the Busch Series."

The driver he became in the Busch Series had a rude introduction to the tour in the season-opening race at Daytona in 1998. His car suffered a broken drive shaft on a pit stop (driver error) and a wild flip on the backstretch (wrong place at the wrong time) on the way to a finish of 37th. Yet he recovered quickly in the next five races—grabbing 16th place at Rockingham, 2nd at Las Vegas, 3rd at Nashville, 10th at Darlington, and 2nd place at Bristol—before getting his first Busch Series win at Texas on April 4, 1998. He then had a total of seven wins that year. Earnhardt Jr. finished his rookie season by winning the Busch Series championship with the team that Steve Park put in victory lane three times the previous season.

Earnhardt Jr. had clearly arrived as a NASCAR star by the time *Circle Track*'s Bob Myers interviewed him during the middle of Earnhardt Jr.'s 1998 rookie season.

DALE EARNHARDT JR.

BY BOB MYERS
From *Circle Track* September, 1998

The Younger Earnhardt Is Making a Name of His Own

This article is an interview of Dale Jr. conducted by Bob Myers.

As Dale Earnhardt's 23-year-old son and driver of the number 3 ACDelco Chevrolet he owns in the NASCAR Busch series, do you feel like you're living in a glass showcase with everybody watching?
Sometimes I do, but I have to concentrate on what's important, and that's the race team.

Obviously you are proud to be an Earnhardt, but is there pressure on you to live up to your father's tradition of excellence?
Not really…I want to be my own person and make a name for myself, but there's no pressure to be as successful as my father.

Do you sometimes wish at the race track that your name wasn't Earnhardt?
No. Some people think there are disadvantages and pressure to being an Earnhardt, but I think there are more advantages than disadvantages.

Do the assets—money, experience, advice—available to you put an extra burden on you to perform?
Naw. It makes it easier. It presents the opportunity to run good. The only thing new about the team that was successful with Steve Park last year is me. We wanted to try to pick up where Steve left off [3 wins, 12 top fives, and 3rd in points].

Moving to the Busch series full-time this year, how did the ride in the number 3 Chevrolet come about?
For a couple years, I had thought about the possibility of driving that car. I don't think dad thought I was ready. Tony Eury [veteran crew chief] and the guys on the team wanted and expected me to drive. There were lengthy discussions and meetings, and I don't think daddy made the decision

A chip off the ol' block: Earnhardt Jr.'s first Busch win came in Texas. *Paul Melhado*

Daddy Dale celebrates at Daytona. *Sam Sharpe*

until a month before the [opening] race at Daytona. And he probably wondered about me during the first three or four races.

What did he tell you at decision time?
He still hasn't told me anything face-to-face. We have no agreement or contract.

After winning your first Busch Grand National [BGN] race, a major one at Texas Motor Speedway in April, in only your 16th BGN start, and after logging four top fives, including two 2nds in eight starts before a wreck and 32nd place at Talladega cost you the points lead, have you exceeded expectations?
So far, on the general timeline, we've accomplished more earlier than I thought we would. I wanted us to be real consistent, but I didn't think that would come three races into the season. I thought I would need more time to build confidence.

Did you expect to win so quickly?
No. But I knew we were capable. We could have won earlier. [He finished second at Las Vegas and Bristol.]

"He has done so much for me in racing and life. I feel compelled to drive for him and try to win as many races and championships as I can, to try to pay him back."
—*Dale Earnhardt Jr. on his father*

"When he has all his little ducks in a row, he doesn't want anybody messing with them. I'm kind of like that," says Dale Earnhardt Jr. *Paul Melhado*

In fact, what are your expectations this year?
To finish in the top five consistently. Do that, and we could win the championship without another win.

Was the warm embrace by your proud dad—reminiscent of golf phenomenon Tiger Woods and his father at the 1997 Masters—after the Texas victory an emotional moment for you?
The most emotional of my life. It stirred memories of the years I had tried so hard to earn my dad's approval. Maybe that did it. It really was a proud moment for him, to show that much excitement and happiness over something that I had accomplished.

Does your father coach you on the radio during races?
Somewhat. He sees opportunities and situations start to develop way before I do. He's been there, done that. He recommended a four-tire final stop in the Texas race, and we decided that was the route to go. That call was a major factor in the win. During the final six laps, the radio was quiet.

You've said your dad's coaching makes you nervous. Why?

Because I know how much he wants me and the team to do well, and because he's my father. I'm constantly concerned about being ridiculed or criticized for something, because I know he is the best, at least in my eyes. It means a lot for me to do well, and hearing him on the radio brings all that to reality. I can get on the race track and forget everything else, but when I hear that voice, I know he's watching my every move.

What's the most important thing he has instilled in you?

Determination and drive.

What did your daddy say to you after you damaged the drive shaft in the pits and then crashed spectacularly during the Daytona 300, the first race of the season?

Nothing. He called on the radio and told us to calm down, just fix the car [drive shaft] and for me to get back in the race for drafting experience. After I crashed, I was sure he was going to chew my head off.

How did you feel after he won the Daytona 500, in his 20th try, the next day?

That was unique. I experienced the same emotions he did, because I knew of all the near misses he had over the years. I will always regret I wasn't there to enjoy it with him, because it's something he really wanted. I watched on television. I had come home because I didn't feel too well after my wreck.

Describe your driving style.

Aggressive, more so at times than it should be, relative to the way NASCAR runs the series. NASCAR is less tolerant of aggressive driving, and you can't be as aggressive as my dad used to be. I enjoy that kind of racing. I hate watching a race that looks like a bunch of toy soldiers marching around. Fans like action, even if their favorite driver gets bumped around or spun out.

Earnhardt Jr. finished 16th in the ACDelco 200 at Rockingham in October of 2000; he carried the ACDelco colors full-time the next season. *Nigel Kinrade*

How much did that first victory mean to you and your team, led by Eury and sponsored primarily by ACDelco?

It meant a lot. It was neat to finally show the ACDelco people that they had made the right decision, to trust a rookie as young as I am. Regarding the team, I grew up with Tony about as much as with my dad. Tony might not realize it, but he taught me a lot and has been a big influence on me. It was cool to win the race as much for him as my dad.

Fresh from the late-model ranks, Earnhardt Jr. hit the Busch Series in 1998. *Harold Hinson*

Were you aware of fans at Texas cheering practically every car you passed and going crazy when you got under Nemechek? If so, how did that make you feel?

Not during the race, but once I got out of the car in victory lane I sure was aware. I'd gotten some idea of how many fans were supporting me from the cheering when drivers rode around the track during introduction. I think we might have picked up a few more fans that day. It was a thrill.

You're always in the spotlight because of your name, but has the media attention increased since your first victory?

Yeah. I'm being pulled right and left.

Do you enjoy, and how important is, media awareness—doing interviews, mixing with fans, and keeping other commitments off the track?

I enjoy autograph sessions the most because I meet the fans, and they are a lot of fun. Even though I am Dale Earnhardt's son, I've always been a big fan. I feel I can relate to fans because they're my kind of people. Some of the other stuff—dinners, parties, and meetings—I'm not too cool about. I'm not much on dressing up, especially in a tuxedo.

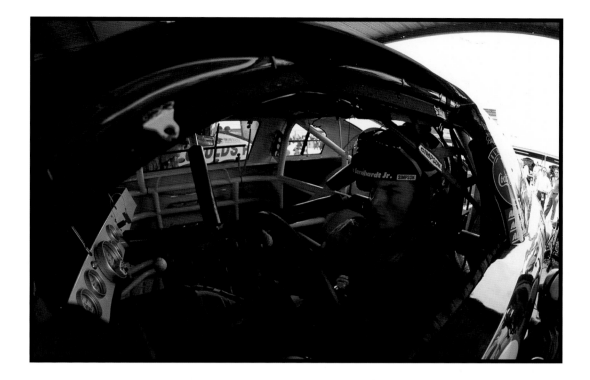

While he waits to turn laps, Earnhardt Jr.'s crew works on the car during his Busch Series debut at Daytona in 1998. *Harold Hinson*

Earnhardt Jr. was strapped in for a Busch Series race at Bristol Motor Speedway in August of 1997. *Harold Hinson*

In 1998, Texas Motor Speedway was the scene of Earnhardt Jr.'s first win in the Busch Series. *Harold Hinson*

After nearly two decades in the spotlight, your father seems to be somewhat shy. Are you that way?
I don't know if it's shy, maybe we just ain't good at putting words together. If we could express ourselves better, without offending anybody, we'd talk and try to get our point across more often. It's so easy to hurt people's feelings.

At 6 feet, 165 pounds, you have your father's build, some of his features, and apparently his racing genes. What other similar attributes do you possess?
I don't know. He's not one who likes to be imitated or copied. If I were to say I am like him in any way in this article, he wouldn't be too happy with me. He's very possessive and territorial. When he has all his little ducks in a row, he doesn't want anybody messing with them. I'm kind of like that.

You don't have his menacing mustache. Do you plan to grow one?

Naw. I don't even know if I can. I might grow a beard during hunting season.

After racing in the Late Model Division of the Winston Racing Series from 1993 to 1996, winning three starts, with 59 top-five and 90 top-ten finishes—and after competing in eight Busch races last year, with a best finish of seventh—were you convinced you were ready for the Busch Series full-time?

Yes. In the Winston Racing Series, I helped put together, worked on, and set up my cars. I learned from my mistakes, and that's paying off now. I wasn't a dominating driver, didn't win many races, but I was consistent.

What's your opinion of Winston Cup drivers competing in Busch races?

I like it. Having a chance to race against them is like taking a class in school. If you're in the top five at the end of a race, you've made an A+ in the class.

Even though your father provided resources and guidance, he didn't serve everything on a silver platter. Haven't you had to work for what you have?

Yeah. He supplied the cars and equipment, but there was sponsorship for the program and everything wasn't out of his pocket. He said, "Here's an opportunity. Here are some cars. Race them. In three years, we'll see how you're doing." At least I learned enough to move to Busch.

Is there a timetable for advancing to Winston Cup?
Not necessarily. What I'll probably do is run two or three more seasons in Busch, at least through 2000, then take the number 3 ACDelco team to Winston Cup. I think the team would be competitive there now.

Would you like to continue driving for your father, particularly after he retires as a driver?
I think so. I believe that's what he'd like me to do. He has done so much for me in racing and life. I feel compelled to drive for him and try to win as many races and championships as I can, to try to pay him back.

How many more years do you think he will drive?
Probably a couple more years, or maybe a year or two after I join Winston Cup.

Do you think about accomplishing what he has: 7 championships, 71 victories, and a motorsports-record $31.8 million in race earnings as of this writing?
Yes. And I think it's possible. The number of races and purses is increasing as Winston Cup grows.

A Busch Series ride at Lowe's Motor Speedway in 1997 bore the number 31 and a resting Earnhardt Jr.
Harold Hinson

You grossed a Series-leading $249,405 in prize money in the first nine BGN races this year. How much does money mean to you?
Not a whole lot, because I don't see much of it. I draw a salary and live on it. Like other drivers, I get a percentage of the race earnings, but that goes into a special account. I don't see that money. I like it that way. I know I have money in the bank to pay my taxes and to invest. Having more money hasn't changed me as a person. That can happen when a pile of money is dumped in your lap.

At what point in early life did you know that you wanted to make racing a career?
Driving race cars was a childhood fantasy. When I was 15, Concord Motor Speedway started a Street Stock Division. A newspaper that was lying on a table in the shop had an ad or story about the new division. I walked in after school and [brother] Kerry was there. Dad pointed to the paper

A year before this 1998 photo was taken at Lowe's Motor Speedway, Earnhardt Jr. was still turning wrenches on his late-model ride. *Nigel Kinrade*

and said, "You boys ought to take a look at that and get interested." That's when I had my first chance. I had wondered for a long time if I could do it. I sold my go-cart for $500, bought a car at a junkyard for $200, and built a race car with the other $300. I was fourth in the first race I ran. Kerry drove the car until I got old enough.

At what age did you start racing go-carts?
When I was 13, and only for a year. My dad didn't like carts because they didn't have seatbelts and roll bars, and I came flying out of them quite often.

Did the fact that you are an Earnhardt influence your decision to race?
Yeah. I saw firsthand how competitive and enjoyable racing was and what it was all about.

Did you tell your father you wanted to race, or did he ask you first?
I had told him a couple of times I wanted to race. When I was 13, I told him I didn't think I would make it to 16, that I just couldn't stand waiting and worrying. He wanted Kerry and me to get involved, but he didn't push us.

Are Kerry and your sister, Kelley, continuing to race?
No.

Tires smoked during a pit stop at Daytona. A broken drive shaft and a wild, tumbling crash on the backstretch spoiled Earnhardt Jr.'s debut at the track.
Nigel Kinrade

The crew made hasty repairs at Talladega after the rookie driver crashed.
Nigel Kinrade

Did you hang around your dad's shop and go to the races when you were a kid?
Yeah. From 1981 until I started driving myself.

Steve Park (right) was the driver for the ACDelco Chevrolet before Earnhardt Jr. (talking to Dick Trickle) took over. *Mike Gurnsey*

What other interests did you have while growing up in Kannapolis, North Carolina?
Practically none.

Where did you attend high school, and did you participate in sports?
I played a little soccer during my second- and ninth-grade years. I went to several schools: Christian, private, and military…because I was a bad little kid. I wanted to drive race cars, not fool around with anything else. A year and a half in a military school did more good for me than anything else. That was a wake-up call. I finally graduated from Mooresville Senior High.

How important is at least a high school education to a race driver?
Very. School is much more than book learning. It teaches you to deal with people, and if you can't do that, you're not going very far in racing.

Where do you reside?
I have a double-wide [mobile home] across the street from the shops. I do the cleaning and laundry. I enjoy working in the yard and have planted some bushes.

Earnhardt Jr. and Dale Jarrett chatted prior to a Busch Series race at Michigan in 1997. Earnhardt Jr. finished seventh—for his best run in seven starts that season—while Steve Park won. *Nigel Kinrade*

What type of person are you?
Real laid-back. I had to develop that style. In the 10th grade, I started getting bad stomach pains. This went on for a time. I worried myself sick about doing well in school and pleasing my father. Two years ago, I quit worrying about a lot of things, particularly what other people thought.

You're single, so does that mean you're an eligible bachelor or do you have a steady girlfriend?
Very eligible.

What leisure activities do you enjoy?
I enjoy hunting once or twice a year, although I'm not into that as much as my father is. I fool around with remote-control cars and play on my computer [for] hours on end.

What sort of lifestyle do you lead?
Very simple, nothing special or fancy. For example, I enjoy riding around in my pickup truck and watching TV. I like jeans, T-shirts, and sneakers, old country and rock-and-roll, solid gold soul, and comedy movies.

Where does your mother, Brenda, reside, do you see her often, and what does she say about your racing?

She has remarried and lives in Norfolk, Virginia. I talk to her on the phone from time to time, and she visits us at least once a year. I love her to death. She's really cool. I lived with her after she and daddy were divorced in 1978, until I came to live with my father and stepmother, Teresa, in 1981. Teresa has been a mother figure to me as well, and I'm grateful to her for everything she has done. A lot of people don't know that Teresa isn't my real mother.

You never knew your late grandfather, Hall of Fame driver Ralph Earnhardt, did you?

No.

Earnhardt Jr. quickly became a fixture in the Busch Series. *Nigel Kinrade*

Is grandmother Martha Earnhardt proud of you?
Oh, yeah. I'm still her little grandson, and she's nervous about me getting hurt. But I think she has more confidence in me now.

Are you concerned about getting hurt?
Naw. Not at all.

Would you say you are very close to your family?
Yes. I've gotten closer in the past couple of years, because I think I've shown them that I'm not the spoiled-rotten kid I was when I was 10–12 years old. That's part of growing up.

Are you generally pleased with your racing career to this point?
I think so. I have a killer instinct to win races, but if I don't win, I won't worry about it. If I finish good enough to make the car owner and sponsor happy, and when I get home have enough money to pay the electrical bill, that's fine with me.

Dale Earnhardt Jr. is shown pausing prior to racing at Lowe's Motor Speedway. *Nigel Kinrade*

What are your goals in racing?
To win a Busch and a Winston Cup championship. And it's important to win a Daytona 300 and a Daytona 500. Anything else will be a bonus.

Anything you wish to add?
I could go on and on about all the people who have helped me get where I am, but there's one I don't want to forget, Gary Hargett. He was my crew chief and mechanic my first three years in late-models, and I raced out of his shop in Marshville, North Carolina [about 35 miles east of Charlotte]. He worked with Harry Gant and my dad in the 1970s. He was the grandfather I never had. When I started driving for him, I was young and self-centered. But he and his volunteer crew gave me no breaks because of who I was. He taught me how to deal with people, how to get people to help you, and how to hold groups together. He used a lot of common sense. One of the hardest things I've done was to leave him. But it was necessary, when space became available, to move my race cars from his shop to my dad's operation in late 1995, so that I could work on them daily and learn more about them.

THE NEXT DALE EARNHARDT

3

From *Stock Car Racing* magazine, September 1998

He's Here, and He's Driving Daddy's Car

There are enough expectations to fill a transporter when you grow up as the namesake of a genuine motorsports icon. When *Stock Car Racing* caught up with Dale Earnhardt Jr. for this September 1998 cover story, he was 23 and had grown accustomed to the baggage that came with being an Earnhardt and driving a stock car for a living. He was also well on his way to carving quite a name for himself as a Busch Series competitor.

By the midpoint of the 1998 season, Earnhardt Jr.'s rookie year in the Busch Series, he had claimed his first two Busch wins, at Texas and Dover, and was in the midst of what would become a seven-win, title-earning campaign. It was quite evident that this kid—one year removed from the late-model ranks—carried more than just his father's name.

Earnhardt Sr. offers a little fatherly advice to his rookie driver. *Nigel Kinrade*

Dale Earnhardt Jr. was born with a surname which symbolizes action and decisiveness. He has done all he can to live up to it, yet he responds to the pressure with surprising patience and maturity.

"It's real early in my career," says Dale Earnhardt Jr. "I think a lot of people need to realize that."

Dale Jr. is but 23 years old, and a few months into the professional phase of his race-driving life. At this young age, he has several memorable performances to his credit. One April Saturday in Texas, he charged from behind after a late pit stop and picked a victory—his first in NASCAR's Busch Series—out of Joe Nemechek's pocket.

And how about Dover at the end of May? That was the race where young Mr. Earnhardt came onto pit road a little too fast, spun his car out of the lead, and then seemed so determined to make up for his blunder that he blew the doors off the rest of the field and won again. Patience, hell.

All Dale Earnhardt Jr. has done in the 1998 season is grab one of the toughest leagues in the sport and wrestle it to the ground. In the season opener at Daytona, he qualified third. Seven races into the schedule, in just his 16th start in the Series, he won at Texas. Dover was this year's start number 13. He has made running up front look like it was his birthright. And maybe it was.

Dale Sr. remembers giving his son this advice: "You don't have to do what I've done. Just go out and do what you can do. Just win races, and you'll do fine." Clearly, Dale Jr. listened. To say that he is doing fine would be the motorsports understatement of 1998.

He has become, hands down, the most popular driver in the Busch division. The official award won't be handed out until season's end, but if you listen to the crowd reaction at any given race you can see that the thing is a lock. And at every stop on the Series, he is the favorite subject of the local media. In fact, the drill for interviewing Dale Earnhardt Jr. at the racetrack has become much the same as it is for interviewing Dale Earnhardt Sr.: make an appointment, show up on time outside his transporter, do your interview, and make room for the next guy. It is the only way everybody will get their shot at him. The Busch Series, which has seen its share of young drivers so eager for ink

There were few—very few—embarrassing moments like this Charlotte spin where Earnhardt Jr. is heading toward the Porta-John. *Dale Grubba*

Earnhardt Jr.'s crew services the car on a pit stop at Atlanta. *Nigel Kinrade*

Earnhardt Jr. leads the pack down the frontstretch in Michigan. The popularity of the third-generation Earnhardt helped fill the grandstands for Busch Series events.
Nigel Kinrade

that they would wax a writer's car in exchange for a story, has never had a newcomer as hot as this one.

Maybe NASCAR hasn't, either. When Jeff Gordon arrived in the Busch Series in 1991, only those who had seen him in open-wheel cars had any real inkling that he was anything special; initially, a lot of stock car folks wrote off Gordon as a wild child who might never stop crashing. Before Jeff, the last wunderkind who generated any real media splash even before he reached the Winston Cup level was Kyle Petty, who was dubbed a "prince"—well, his father was a King—by the full-time beat writers after his 1979 ARCA [Automobile Race Car Association] victory at Daytona. But face it, you could seat all of those full-time beat writers in a pretty small pressroom in 1979.

Dale Earnhardt Jr. comes into the spotlight at a time when NASCAR has never been bigger, and he comes bearing its biggest name. Life as a "son of" is never easy and being Billy Earnhardt or Bobby Earnhardt would have been tough enough. Being Dale Jr., however, has to represent a whole

different level of tough. Fortunately, it was hung on a pretty tough specimen; when I inquire about the burden of his name, he says, "It's never really been a problem."

Dad looked on proudly in 1998 while Earnhardt Jr. was being interviewed after an exhibition race against Jeremy Mayfield at Lowe's Motor Speedway. *Harold Hinson*

"You don't ever feel like it's a lot to live up to?" I ask.

"No. I mean, I know I'm only going to be as good as I can be. All I can do is go out there and do my best."

He shoots a grin, which is not unlike his daddy's, slightly crooked and full of confidence, and reminds me that after 23 years, he has sort of gotten used to being Dale Earnhardt Jr.

"I don't know any different," he says.

The grin is not all that these Earnhardts have in common. On the youngster's best days, when he races with the blend of brains and brawn that he displayed at Texas and Dover, their driving styles look almost interchangeable.

"He's a competitive little driver," says the father of the son. "He likes to get aggressive."

The only problem, according to Dale Sr., is that there are days when the boy's maturity is still a lap down to his desire. He points to the springtime events at Nazareth and Charlotte, and says, "He had the best race car two races in a row, and he wrecked it two races in a row. You've got to be able to be aggressive and use your head, too."

That is enough to raise the eyebrows of Tony Eury, crew chief for the Busch Series arm of Dale Earnhardt, Inc. Eury has chummed around with Dale Sr. forever, "I was probably 11 or 12 when I met him," and they were working together on Earnhardt's short-track cars as long ago as 1976. He has

Earnhardt Jr. and Matt Kenseth became friends while competing in the Busch Series. They're shown before the next-to-last race of the season at Atlanta in November 1998. Earnhardt Jr. edged Kenseth for the Busch Series title by 48 points one week later. *Nigel Kinrade*

known Dale Jr. quite literally since his birth in October of 1974. If anybody on the planet qualifies as an expert on drivers named Dale Earnhardt, it is Eury.

"A lot of people think Dale Jr. is a hard racer," Eury says. "But when his daddy first started, he was worse."

The elder Earnhardt, Eury claims, ". . . was his own worst enemy. He probably should have won a lot more races than he did [in the beginning], but he tore up his equipment before the end of the race."

Those long-ago mistakes, blurred as they were by Earnhardt's 1980s rise to big-league glory, were not forgotten by the man who made them. They became, Eury believes, part of Dale Jr.'s education: "His daddy has told him about all that stuff," the mechanic says.

The lessons took hold. Dale Sr.'s protests aside, young Earnhardt has gotten himself into no more trouble than several other fast Busch Series rookies have over the past few seasons.

"I'll get a little aggressive when the situation calls for it," Junior says. "But I try to be patient as much as I possibly can."

Dale Earnhardt Jr., at 23, is in many ways older and wiser than his dad was at the same age. If anything, he resembles the racer Dale Sr. became more than the racer Dale Sr. used to be. Sometimes the similarities are eerie.

"I haven't tried to raise him to be like me," the father says when I ask about this. "I've tried to raise him to be his own person."

In that, he has succeeded; it's just that the person Dale Jr. became has an awful lot in common with Dale Sr. Both of them stick close to their cars and their teams at the track, focusing on the job at hand and only occasionally socializing with competitors. Both of them have an uncanny ability to isolate themselves in a crowd; even as nosey onlookers besiege their garage stalls, they seem somehow alone at the center of it all. Both of them are essentially shy, and during interviews they often seem worried that they are giving too much of themselves away.

> "You don't have to do what I've done. Just go out and do what you can do. Just win races, and you'll do fine."
> —*Dale Earnhardt Sr. to Earnhardt Jr.*

Earnhardt Jr. insists that there are plenty of differences between them, and that one reason he has been doing so many interviews is "so people can see more of my personality. Because whatever they don't know about me, they assume it's pretty close to what Dad is like."

But even as his own persona emerges, there is no escaping the fact that it really is pretty close to his dad's. Exhibit A: I am pressing Dale Jr. about the ways in which he and his father are alike, and he says, "We both like to get away, like to be left alone. Have a good, peaceful day by yourself, you know? We're very, uh, independent."

That brings to mind something I heard Dale Sr. say years ago about his own father, the late NASCAR sportsman champ Ralph Earnhardt. "He was pretty independent, pretty quiet, did his own thing," Dale Sr. said that day. "He wasn't the type who depended on too many other people."

So maybe all of it, including the talent and the independence, is in the Earnhardt genes, passed down from Ralph to Dale to Dale Jr. In his most open moments, Dale Sr. will fondly recall sitting in the grandstands at various Carolina bullrings, watching Ralph Earnhardt work his magic in traffic, and then quizzing him about his winning moves. Dale Jr. has heard and read those stories enough to have developed his own questions about Ralph Earnhardt, who died the year before the youngest Earnhardt was born.

"I'm interested in what kind of person he was," Junior says. "You know, what kind of personality he had, whether he was outspoken or not, things like that. I like to find out about that as much as I can."

I ask Dale Jr., "Do you think you studied your father as closely as he studied his?"

He sighs. "I don't know for sure how closely he studied ol' Ralph. But I've paid a lot of attention to Dad. I've watched him make good moves and bad moves, and I've tried to learn from both."

Curious, I throw the same question to Dale Sr.: Does he suppose his son watched him the way he watched his own dad? I am surprised to catch Earnhardt looking rather curious himself.

"I don't know, really," he says.

Now there is a hint of melancholy on the champion's face. He says, "I went to the races and watched my dad week after week, and Dale Jr. has done that, too. But I hung around the shop more when I was a kid than Dale Jr. did."

True enough: Dale Jr. had a much different childhood than his father did. Dad grew up knee-deep in race car parts, tagging after Ralph. Junior was born when Dale Earnhardt was flat broke and finding wedded bliss as elusive as racing success. "I struck out on marriage a couple times," says Dale Sr. Little E was relegated by his parents' divorce to the fringes of the sport. Living with his mother, his first exposure to racing consisted of listening to events on the radio, "probably in 1978. Dad was getting just a couple starts in Winston Cup."

He says quietly, "It was kind of tough being away from him."

It wasn't until 1982, when Dale Sr. had become a NASCAR hero, married his third and present wife Teresa, and assumed custody of Dale Jr., that his son "got the chance to be around him, and find out more about what he was like."

The number 3 was a natural fit for the son of the man who made the number synonymous with hard driving and stock car success. *Nigel Kinrade*

It was no surprise that he chose to answer the family calling. Junior's first race came in a go-cart "when I was about 12." The next step was a "celebrity" race in Legends cars at Charlotte, running against the offspring of some of his dad's Winston Cup rivals. By 1994, at age 19, he was a regular in NASCAR's late-model stock car class. His home track was South Carolina's Myrtle Beach Speedway, but before long he branched out, hopscotching around the region "just to learn about different bankings, different [track] lengths, different speeds, different corner entries and exits."

I say to Junior, "Could you tell right away that you had the ingredients to be good?"

He gives me his daddy's crooked and confident grin again, "Yeah. I knew I could drive a good car well."

The job of keeping young Earnhardt in good cars initially fell to Gary Hargett, a veteran wrench who years earlier had labored on Dale Sr.'s Saturday-night specials. In Hargett, Junior found a mentor: "I was just a wild buck, but he taught me about race cars, taught me how to handle myself, taught me how to work with people."

This was, as you might guess, part of a plan. Dale Sr. says, "When I started, I drove for other guys, too. I had already learned a lot by working with Dad, but there's still that learning process where you need to find things out for yourself by working with different people like Dale Jr. did."

It helped young Earnhardt the same way it helped Dale Sr.: the more he learned, the faster he got, and the more he learned.

He remembers nights making his first big chassis decisions himself, running great, and thinking, "Hey, I'm getting a hold of this." Soon, after learning by a method Dale Sr. refers to as "trial and error, learn-as-you-go," Junior was calling his own shots.

This was Earnhardt's way of dropping the boy out of the nest. He had taken the same tack with his oldest son Kerry (now 28) and daughter Kelley (25) when they began racing late-models a few years earlier; all three kids worked on their own cars. In fact, all three kids worked, period, because Dale Earnhardt did not believe in free rides. If his children wanted to go racing, that was fine, but they would have to earn their keep while they did so. They could hire on at one of the family businesses, or they could find jobs elsewhere, but they were damn sure going to work.

"I wanted them to be able to handle their own affairs," Dale Sr. says. "I wanted them to be able to handle life."

Although not as intimidating as his father's black number 3 Chevrolet, Earnhardt Jr.'s blue number 3 led the Busch Series in wins (7) and money won ($837,065) in 1998.
Nigel Kinrade

Richard Childress offers advice prior to Earnhardt Jr.'s debut at Daytona. *Harold Hinson*

Junior landed in the service department at Dale Earnhardt Chevrolet and supported his late-model Chevy by performing oil changes on the local citizenry's Cavaliers and Caprices.

Today, Dale Jr. has what he calls "a lot of respect" for Dad's earn-your-keep approach to raising children and race drivers.

"When it was going on, I didn't like it much. But it is the best way. It makes me take a lot of pride in my racing, and a lot of pride in what I've done."

He pauses. "And a lot of pride in why I'm sitting here."

He means, of course, sitting in the DEI fleet of Busch cars. He had been around those cars for years, had watched Jeff Green and then Steve Park drive them, and, as any racer would, had longed to drive them himself. But his father's no-free-ride policy stood: simply being an Earnhardt didn't entitle you to the keys of the family Busch cars.

"I didn't know if I was ever going to get the chance [to move up]," Junior says.

But the chance did come, in June of 1996 at Myrtle Beach.

"That was a place he had run a lot," Dale Sr. says, "so we felt it would be a good opportunity for him to get some experience in these Busch cars."

Tony Eury Sr., uncle to Earnhardt Jr., provided a steady hand during their first season together in the Busch Series and later moved up to Winston Cup with Earnhardt Jr. *Nigel Kinrade*

Green was the team's lead driver at the time, and Dale Jr.'s ride was little more than a decent backup. But he qualified 7th and, after spinning early on and losing a lap, soldiered home 14th, a result which didn't come close to reflecting the show he put on.

"We passed cars all race long," Junior says. "We could have maybe finished in the lead lap, but I wasn't running for points, so I never got up to the front of the [restart] line under caution. I stayed in the back, out of everybody's way. Then I'd pass 'em again. It was like we passed everybody there, over and over."

His father watched it on television from Michigan, where he was running in a Winston Cup race the next day. Seeing his son blow past some of the toughest racers in the Busch Series, he says with a gleam in his eye, "was a good feeling."

Good enough, apparently, to book the lad for eight Busch events in 1997, beside the team's rookie star Steve Park. Junior's starts came at tracks ranging from the Nashville half-miler to the Watkins Glen road course and the 2-mile California Speedway. It was, Dale Earnhardt admits, an audition: "We were trying to give him a feel for [the series], and give ourselves a feel for him." On the strength of a seventh-place finish at Michigan, an outside-pole qualifying run at Bristol, and a top-ten start at the Glen, Junior passed.

Tony Eury says, "He never had the kind of equipment we had for Steve; Dale Jr. always had the second-best car, always had an engine that wasn't as good as ours, always worked on it himself, just him and a couple of young guys from his late-model team. But he managed to be pretty competitive."

Along the way, Park won three races and became the obvious choice to drive the new Winston Cup entry DEI would field in 1998. That left an open seat in the Busch car. Dale Sr. says, "We were like, 'OK, do we put in someone with experience, or do we take a chance with somebody new?' We had taken chances with Jeff Green and Steve Park, and they both did a good job. So we said, 'We'll just take a chance on Dale Jr., too.'"

Junior jumped at the offer. "I knew the team was capable," he says, "because they won with Steve. I knew all the ingredients were there to run well. We just had to find out whether I could do it."

I ask him if he wasn't just a little bit nervous about the whole thing, and he shoots back a look that tells me exactly how dumb a question this is.

"Of course I was nervous. But I wasn't going to turn it down."

The move put him under the watchful eye of Eury, who is schooling Dale Jr. just as Gary Hargett did in the late-model days. It also teamed him with Eury's son Tony Jr., who, in addition to being the team's chassis specialist, happens to be a cousin of Dale Jr.'s.

"They kinda hang out together," Eury Sr. says, "and they trust each other a lot, which is good."

At Daytona, their first race as a team, they qualified behind only Mike McLaughlin and Joe Nemechek, two superspeedway veterans. In the race, Dale Jr. ran with the leaders until he broke a drive shaft leaving the pits and lost several laps. Later, while logging miles to pad his experience, he got caught up in a backstretch tangle and flipped. Unfazed, he said, "We practiced good, qualified good, raced good, drafted good. But circumstances got us."

Circumstances couldn't get him every week. At Las Vegas, the kid ran a great 2nd to Jimmy Spencer; at Nashville he was a fighting 3rd; at tricky Darlington, a solid 10th; and at Bristol, he trailed only Elliott Sadler at the finish after starting from the pole.

Then came Texas, where he seemed to have lost any hope of winning when he stopped for tires late in the race, with Nemechek looking like the class of the field. But as Dale Jr. stormed back, every move he made suggested that he would be heard from before the checkered flag fell. And he was: when he caught Nemechek on the next-to-last lap and closed right up on the leader's bumper, using one of his dad's aerodynamic ploys to loosen up Nemechek's

car, it was clear that Junior had decided he wasn't about to run second.

"We came off [turn] two, and we gained on Nemechek a little bit. I could see his car was out of shape; he wasn't very comfortable. Then, off four, we got a run on him, and I knew we'd be able to make a pass on the front straightaway.

"I went to the inside and got by him before we got to the corner, so we could get into the corner good and straight. I knew then that if I held my line and ran as hard as I could, we had a win."

"I want to be my own person and make a name for myself, but there's no pressure to be as successful as my father," —Earnhardt Jr. *Nigel Kinrade*

Strapped in and ready to do battle on Bristol's tough half-mile.
Harold Hinson

His father was in victory lane even before Dale Jr. climbed out of the car, and their initial exchange— Dad leaning into the cockpit for a private word, the son tousling the old man's hair—will play on videotape as long as Junior races.

I ask Dale Earnhardt about that, and about the first words he said to his son. I expect him to either rerun the moment with great emotion, or tell me it is none of my business. Instead, he shrugs. "Just 'Good job, son. Great race. Congratulations.' Something like that."

Turns out Dale Jr. doesn't know for sure, either. "You know, I couldn't really hear him at the time, for all that was going on. But I knew he was happy."

Now things have been pretty much happy ever since. Sure, Junior has made mistakes—including those two straight wrecks his father complains about—but he has run more good races than bad ones. He has listened to Eury, listened to his dad, listened to Steve Park ("He's been really good about giving me advice," Dale Jr. says), and done a remarkable job of reading tracks he has never seen and competitors he has rarely faced.

Maybe the best example was the June race at Richmond. He lost the lead late in the going to Jeff Burton, who had the faster car, but then clung to Burton's tail and kept the outcome in doubt until the last lap. It was his first start at Richmond, and his first prolonged head-to-head scrap with a Winston Cup winner.

"Earnhardt did a super job," Burton said. "He ran me to death."

Tony Eury says, "We knew from last year that Dale Jr. was good. But I don't think we knew he was this good."

There is a chuckle here from Eury, who has now been down the road to stardom with two Dale Earnhardts. He says, "You know, Dale Jr. gets a little wild sometimes on the racetrack, and we've got to calm him down. But it's a lot easier to get that attitude out of a driver than it is to put it in one."

His father's legendary intensity showed in Earhardt Jr. at Charlotte in October of 1998. *Nigel Kinrade*

Meanwhile, Dale Jr.—that "competitive little driver"—continues to gain attention wherever he goes. Every time you turn on one of those weekly motorsports TV programs, some commentator is gushing over him. Every time you flip open the local newspaper on a Busch Series race day, you see his photo on the lead sports page. He is young, he is fast, and he is Dale Earnhardt Jr.

I ask him if he thinks he will ever be fully out of the shadow cast by his own name, and Junior frowns.

"Maybe one day, when Dad retires," he says quietly. "Maybe."

Now he is back to preaching patience, restraint. He says it is a mistake for people to expect him "to be awesome right out of the box." Even his famous father, he points out, needed time to become the Dale Earnhardt we know today. "They forget about the years when he struggled, when he didn't win many races, and he wasn't considered the best."

But that was then, this is now. There is no way to compare their situations, because so much is different: Dale Earnhardt had room to grow in those struggling years because his father, while a great champion, lived and died when NASCAR was essentially a Southern sporting phenomenon; Dale Earnhardt Jr., on the other hand, showed up as the son of a mainstream American icon. Like Hank Williams Jr., he was a household name before he knew it. It would be nice to think that stock car racing might grant young Dale some breathing space, but it just isn't going to happen.

He talks of the responsibilities his father has, the sponsor commitments and the businesses and the other demands, and he says, "It would be tough to be in his shoes. That's not something I'm looking forward to."

I mention this comment to Dale Sr., who says with a laugh, "It's going to happen. As your career grows, as it builds, all that stuff comes with the territory. It won't be a thing where he can say, 'I don't want to do this.' Because there's no way you can't."

"So you think he'll grow into those responsibilities," I ask, "the same way you did?"

Cameramen, reporters, or requests for interviews were never far away during Earnhardt Jr.'s rookie season in the Busch Series. *Stock Car Racing Archives*

Earnhardt the father says, "He'll have to, if he's going to make it in this business."

Maybe it is happening without the kid even seeing it. When my time with him is done, I step out of his team's transporter and recognize a couple of daily writers standing around, waiting their turn. Without even knowing it, I catch myself thinking, he is growing into those shoes.

Dale Earnhardt likes to say of his boy, "In a year or two, once when we get some time on him, he'll be OK."

Look again, Dad. Junior is OK right now.

4

LIVING UP TO THE HYPE

BY BRUCE MARTIN
From *Stock Car Racing*, August 1999

An Almost Cultlike Following

Has High Expectations for Little E

Dale Earnhardt Jr. was focused on winning another Busch Series title in 1999, but there was another goal to be reckoned with: the five Winston Cup events his team planned as a prelude to its Cup rookie season in 2000. The buildup began early in 1999, with tracks at Charlotte, New Hampshire, Michigan, Richmond, and Atlanta chosen as the first five venues in his Cup career.

No rookie driver in NASCAR Winston Cup history has entered his first race with as many expectations, or as much hype, as Dale Earnhardt Jr. The attention that has been placed on the 24-year-old son of Dale Earnhardt is far greater than that for the late Davey Allison, or even for Jeff Gordon. And compared to the buildup for young Earnhardt's first race, Tony Stewart's debut in the Daytona 500 may have well happened in relative obscurity.

But is there any way that Dale Earnhardt Jr. can ever live up to that much hype?

"This is just rolling along and snowballing and we're going to see how far down the hill is," Earnhardt Jr. says. "I hope it keeps going for a long time. I didn't expect it to happen, but it's happening.

"I don't know whether to slow it down, to stop it for a minute, to take a break, to keep going, to speed it up. I don't really know because I don't have any experience with this. My father seems to think that more is better or more demand is better. The dogs are howling at the gate and he keeps on letting them in. Anytime anybody beats on the door, he keeps letting them in. That's cool, I guess, if that's the way it needs to be.

Being a NASCAR star means making appearances of all types, including making sales pitches. *Nigel Kinrade*

The red Budweiser Chevrolet was about to become a fixture in the Winston Cup garage. *Harold Hinson*

"You feel like everybody's looking at you. You feel like all eyes are on you."

Armed with a lucrative sponsorship from Budweiser, a famous father who is also his team owner, and the 1998 Busch Series championship earned in his first full season, the unassuming Earnhardt has created an almost cultlike following.

"The swarms are fun," Earnhardt says. "It's like at Atlanta, trying to go to driver's introduction last year. Those times are hilarious. They're great. I feel like a rock star every once in a while. It's kind of fun. At least you get to experience what they go through sometimes."

Son of The Intimidator

"I wish everybody could see me now," says the junior Earnhardt.

Especially those he went to high school with. As a youngster, his father shipped him and his sister Kelley off to Oak Ridge Military Academy near Greensboro, North Carolina. Young Dale learned a great deal of discipline before he returned to public school at Mooresville High School, but being the son of a famous father often had its drawbacks.

As he began his transition into Winston Cup, Dale Earnhardt Jr. found himself at the center of attention. *Harold Hinson*

"I had an interesting time going through high school," Earnhardt recalls. "I was kind of a loner during that period of my life. I was driving race cars and I guess that wasn't cool to a lot of the other high school kids. Being Dale Earnhardt's son wasn't an advantage, I'll tell you that. It was a disadvantage the majority of times. If he ran good, nobody ever said anything to you, but if he ran bad, you got picked on.

"I didn't understand why my father was booed so much, but I felt like at the time he was standing up for what he felt was right and that's real important.

"When I was in school, there were jealous kids. There were kids that never said anything to you when your dad won a race, but when he crashed out, they were the first ones to say, 'So, your daddy wrecked!' You learn to deal with that at an early age."

It was also while young Earnhardt was away at military school that his father was becoming the biggest name in NASCAR Winston Cup racing. This was at the peak of Earnhardt's career, when he intimidated opponents and won Winston Cup titles on a regular basis.

During Earnhardt's dominance, the sport enjoyed a tremendous spurt in growth, which kept Earnhardt away from home for sponsorship appearances and other demands on his time. Because of that, Dale Jr. was unable to spend a great deal of time with his father.

"The fact my dad wasn't with me when I was growing up, that's all right," Earnhardt says. "Who wants to be around his dad all day, every day? How many butt whippings can one person stand in one week?"

Earnhardt Jr. kept pushing his Busch efforts in 1999 with the knowledge that five Winston Cup races loomed large in his future. *Paul Melhado*

Media Star

Dale Earnhardt Jr. is a breath of fresh air in the Winston Cup garage area. Unlike Gordon and Stewart, who have come from outside of NASCAR's grass roots to become young heroes, Earnhardt appeals to the people who rooted for his father and at the same time portrays an image that major corporations can turn into an icon.

At only 24 years of age, he's almost too naive to realize how much he is in demand, but he does his best to give interviews, answer questions, and chat with the media. And when he talks, he sounds like Boomhauer from the TV cartoon *King of the Hill.*

All of this success came as a huge surprise to Earnhardt's grandmother, Martha. Despite the tremendous success of her late husband, Ralph Earnhardt, and her son, Dale Sr., she didn't expect the same from grandson Dale Jr.

"I haven't talked to her much about it," Dale Jr. says. "She was just surprised I was a race car driver. She didn't think I was going to make one. She didn't have much faith in me. I guess I don't look like I can get out of the rain."

Hard to believe, however, is that young Earnhardt can still enjoy a certain degree of anonymity, simply because the Busch Series drivers aren't as readily recognized as the Winston Cup stars. But Earnhardt also understands it's merely a matter of time before the fans will be able to pick him out of a crowd.

"I can pretty much still do whatever I want, whenever I want, when they give me the time to do it," Earnhardt says. "I think I get a half-day a week now. I'm already complaining about the time I don't have. Isn't that bad?

"I don't see why my dad doesn't like all that attention. You can be a regular guy at the house by yourself. When I was a little kid and I watched people give a race driver attention, I was like, 'Cool, man. That's awesome.' That's always the way I was. I think some people are like that and some people aren't. When people come up to me and say, 'You're one of my favorites,' I'm kind of shocked and surprised because I don't call myself a great race car driver yet."

Countdown to E Day

During his father's dominance, young Earnhardt always watched his father race at Charlotte Motor Speedway; back in those days racetracks were named after the towns they were located near, not by the company that paid the most money for naming rights.

Solitary moments at a racetrack, like this one at California Speedway, were few. *Jon Fitzsimmons*

Dale Earnhardt Jr. in his Winston Cup racing suit.
Harold Hinson

"We had a little area on top of one of the turns in the infield where our family parked, my dad's brothers and our own little group," Dale Jr. recalls. "We'd pitch a few tents and roll our little models and cars down the hill of the road course during the race. We just had a lot of fun. I remember doing that all the time."

As a youngster, Dale Jr. often dreamed that it was him in the race car as he rolled the cars down homemade speedways carved out of the infield at Charlotte Motor Speedway while his father did the real thing a few hundred yards away on the asphalt surface of the racetrack. That's why it is only fitting that young Earnhardt's first attempt at a NASCAR Winston Cup race was set for the Coca-Cola 600 on May 30. To capitalize on his dramatic debut, the team and sponsor even started a "Countdown to E Day" promotion. At one point, Dale Jr. began to call it "Countdown to Hell Day."

Talk about a lot of pressure to make the field for a NASCAR Winston Cup debut.

"I don't think there will be much pressure," Earnhardt says. "I'm going to be excited because I'll be at a Cup race for one. A real, legitimate Cup race, not a make-believe Japan Cup race. It will be a real Cup race where I'll be racing against the best and we'll truly see what I've got. If I have a car that can do that, we'll be there.

"We have the outlook of just taking the bull by the horns and we have a great opportunity to reap the benefits of all the hard work. For years and years, I've worked on trying to be a good race car driver. We had an excellent year last year and we sold a lot of souvenirs. We got a lot of fans interested and that helped my fans a lot.

"You just don't see that kind of reaction to a Busch driver."

Earnhardt got a sneak peek at Winston Cup competition last November when he competed in an exhibition race at the Twin Ring Motegi oval in Japan. It was a race that was highlighted when he ran into the back of his father's car a few times toward the end of the race and eventually passed him to finish sixth—two positions ahead of the seven-time Winston Cup champion.

Rather than beaming proudly and saying, "That's my boy!" the elder Earnhardt was red-faced and thought his namesake should respect his elders.

"Building up to the Japan race, he started considering me more of his competition, like just another guy for him to outrun," Dale Jr. says. "Around that area, he just started spending more time doing other things. I haven't seen him or talked to him much ever since.

Anticipation for Earnhardt Jr.'s move into Winston Cup was growing. *Nigel Kinrade*

The defending Busch Series champion and the defending Winston Cup champion, Jeff Gordon, spent time together at Lowe's Motor Speedway in 1999. *Nigel Kinrade*

Following 1999's final race, at Homestead on November 14, Earnhardt Jr. celebrated his second Busch title and displayed the trophies from both championship seasons.
Nigel Kinrade

"It felt good to beat my dad at Japan because he didn't think I could do it. He always doesn't think I can do it and I like to prove it to him. When you do succeed, he still says, 'I could have done it better.' Or, 'No, you didn't do what you think you did. You're not as big as you think [you] are.'

"He always has some way of putting you down. That makes me keep crawling to get to the top. As long as he keeps acting like he acts, I'll keep acting like I act."

Perhaps it's Earnhardt's way of showing his son "tough love," but he has taken an almost critical approach to how he will treat his son on the racetrack.

"I'll race him just as hard as anyone else," Earnhardt says. "I'm not going to take it easy on him. But hopefully, in the end, it will be Earnhardt and Earnhardt. I'm racing for Richard Childress Racing and racing to win. Whoever else is out there, I'm racing to beat them.

"He has to get in and get started first. He's just a Busch Grand National driver now. We're not worried about him until he gets there."

Rather than be hurt at the way his father responds, Dale Jr. realizes he's being taught a lesson.

"He does make a point of making it as difficult and as much of a struggle as possible," the young Earnhardt says. "He goes out of his way to make things more difficult because he believes, in the long run, I'll be a better person for it.

"I think he is the best ever, but I can sort of understand how he's feeling. You don't want to be outrun by somebody you raised and who is not supposed to know what he's doing or be competitive.

"He's never been one to compliment me often. It's not that he never does, it just makes you insist on always trying to impress him. When you win a race, you do it also for your father, to make him happy because that's something he did a lot. When you do something that he did and not really match his success, but make a leap toward it, that kind of means a lot. Until you succeed or do

Earnhardt Jr. filled many autograph requests in 1999.
Nigel Kinrade

something that he has done or something he's proud of, you never feel up to par. You never feel like you're playing with a full deck.

"Hopefully, I'll win the Daytona 500 before my 20th try. I'm not out to match his accomplishments or anything like that. I just want to be competitive, content, and satisfied with what I'm doing. I'm excited, proud, surprised. You can write the list and check them off."

High Expectations

Earnhardt began his professional driving career at the age of 17, competing in the Street Stock division at Concord Speedway in Concord, North Carolina. Within two seasons, Earnhardt had perfected his driving abilities and joined the NASCAR Late Model Stock division. He ran his first NASCAR Busch Grand National Series event in 1996 at Myrtle Beach, South Carolina. In the Busch Series last season, Earnhardt won more races, led more laps, led more miles, won more money and more poles than any other driver on the circuit this year.

Don Hawk, president of Dale Earnhardt, Inc., and one of the top businessmen in NASCAR Winston Cup racing, negotiated the Budweiser deal. Hawk says the team had high expectations for Earnhardt's first year in Busch Grand National racing, but admits the young driver exceeded those expectations.

"He went a little further than we thought, so that escalated the hype on him," Hawk says. "What we're doing in the Busch Series is what the 24 car [Jeff Gordon] has done in the Winston Cup series and we are moving the bar to the next level.

"He's only 24. The first time his daddy bent a steering wheel in Winston Cup, he was 27. Jeff Gordon has just turned 27. The key on Dale Jr. is he has a contract for five Winston Cup races next year, and five more years on top of that. When that contract is over with, he'll be one year older than his daddy was when he first bent a steering wheel and only one year older than Jeff Gordon is now.

"We're sitting on a 24-year-old keg of dynamite," says Hawk.

With so much happening so soon in his career, how will Dale Earnhardt Jr. keep from being overwhelmed from all the attention when he moves up to Winston Cup?

The September 11, 1999 night race at Richmond was one of the five Winston Cup events Earnhardt Jr. ran that season. He finished 10th after winning Richmond's Busch race the night before. *Nigel Kinrade*

What's better than winning a championship? Winning a second one ranks high on the list. *Nigel Kinrade*

"I've kept a level head through all of this and that comes from living in a double-wide, driving dirty pickup trucks," Earnhardt says. "That's what it's all about.

"Now, maybe Daddy will raise my allowance. I'm just going to be myself and do what I want to do. We don't want to get overwhelmed by all of this. We're lucky, very lucky, and we're blessed. Being in racing with my dad has brought us closer together because it's allowed us to spend more time with each other. That's pretty cool."

Dale Earnhardt Sr. and wife Teresa helped celebrate the second Busch Series title, secured at Phoenix in the penultimate race of the season. *Nigel Kinrade*

Gordon vs. Junior

Having one of the greatest drivers in racing history as his father is perhaps preparing Dale Jr. for an even bigger nemesis in the future—Jeff Gordon. This is the battle that race fans and the media have been looking forward to, although Tony Stewart may be in a position to crash the party with his fantastic rookie season. The Gordon foes are looking for a hero that can knock Gordon off his throne as the top driver in racing today.

Racing fans' hopes have created even more expectations for young Earnhardt.

At Darlington in March, Earnhardt Jr. grabbed a moment to himself. *Nigel Kinrade*

The media blitz was on with Earnhardt Jr.'s Winston Cup debut at Charlotte in May of 1999. *Nigel Kinrade*

A win at Dover in June 1999 kicked off a celebration.
Nigel Kinrade

"I'm ready to take on Jeff and everybody else out there," Earnhardt says. "I've actually had a lot of people talking to me about racing Jeff Gordon. For anybody even thinking I might be able to compete with Jeff Gordon is a compliment because he's the best out there at this moment.

"Me and Jeff have talked about it briefly. It's going to fill the seats a little bit if he has somebody racing him hard and doing it every week and battling for the championship."

Rather than flinch from the challenge, Gordon welcomes the competition that Dale Earnhardt Jr. will provide. Perhaps he needs that to stay motivated in a sport he has dominated unlike any other driver in the sport's history at such an early age.

"I think we all respect him," Gordon says. "He's got a lot of talent. I think just gaining the experience in the heavier Winston Cup cars is the only thing I see he's lacking in. But from what he's done in the Busch Grand National cars, that's not going to take him long to do in the Winston Cup cars.

The official celebration for the team's second straight Busch title came at Homestead in the tour's final race of the season. *Nigel Kinrade*

"There's no doubt, there's always going to be somebody younger, more talented. I've been saying for a long time, they are out there. It's just some of these car owners need to look a little bit harder or take a chance, like Rick Hendrick did with me. Now we're starting to see some real talent stepping up that everybody sees, like Dale Earnhardt Jr. and Matt Kenseth. There are a lot of guys all over the country that we don't get to see that have far more talent than those guys. They just don't get the opportunity to show it.

"Dale Earnhardt Jr. is doing an unbelievable job. I look forward to seeing him come in. He'll be successful because Dale will make sure he is in good equipment, safe equipment, and that is an important part of it. And he's brought him up right. There are some things that I missed out on that you can't do over again, and that's learning more about a stock car before I was able to get to Winston Cup. For me, I learned all about midget and sprint cars, but all of a sudden, I'm in a stock car and I'm learning how to drive it. They were able to learn the stock cars before they ever got to Winston Cup."

Rock Star

Earnhardt is so young, so new to all of this, that he often does a double take when he sees a race fan wearing a T-shirt with his picture on it and cheering him on.

A second successful Busch season firmly established
Earnhardt Jr. as a NASCAR star. *Nigel Kinrade*

Earnhardt Jr. and the ACDelco team looked super
again in 1999. *Nigel Kinrade*

Dad's International Race Of Champions victory at Daytona in February brought a plain-clothes visit to victory lane.
Nigel Kinrade

The Bud Chevrolet looks low and lean during the team's second Cup appearance of the season in July at Loudon. *Nigel Kinrade*

How do you celebrate a Busch Series title? With Busch beer, of course. *Nigel Kinrade*

Earnhardt Jr. looked spiffy in his new Bud duds at Michigan in August. *Nigel Kinrade*

As defending Busch champion, Earnhardt Jr. earned a spot in the 1999 IROC series. *Nigel Kinrade*

"It feels good, but there's never enough, though—you always want more," Earnhardt Jr. says. "There's always a race fan walking by with a Rusty Wallace T-shirt on and you wish he had yours on.

Bill France (second from right) and Dale Earnhardt Sr. shared the spotlight at Homestead during the celebration for the Busch championship. *Nigel Kinrade*

"By being myself and doing the best I can on the track, race fans pay a lot of attention to your personality because that's something that's hard to see. You have to pay attention to what you do on and off the racetrack. If you do the right things, and say the right things, and try to be true and honest to the race fan, he's going to go over there and grab your hat off the shelf. That's what I try to do.

"I can't grow up any faster than I am right now. I'm finding out a lot of new things about myself. Yes, I'm still young."

His youth and inexperience are reasons why he believes he will have no trouble adapting to the Winston Cup Series after being an instant hit in the Busch Series.

"I expect to qualify for the five races and not have to go home from them," Earnhardt says. "I expect to be able to lead a couple of them. I expect to be competitive in all of them.

"The fact that I'm young is probably an advantage. I probably have no clue or idea what's really going on. Somebody told me after we won the Busch championship that it would be 10 years down the road before I really realized what I had accomplished.

"I don't think there's going to be much of a transition. The hard part is going to be juggling the two schedules this year. Even with five races, it's going to be tough on the crew and me. I went to Japan and drove a Winston Cup car. It might not have had the most horsepower or it might not have been the best race car, but I didn't see much difference.

Earnhardt Jr. won the Busch race at Michigan in August of 1999, besting Winston Cup regulars Jeff Gordon, Mark Martin, Jeff Burton, and Michael Waltrip. *Nigel Kinrade*

"I want to win. That's what we came here for. We've probably got a long way to go and a lot of things to figure out before we're at the level of Jeff Gordon and a lot of these other guys. And I understand that."

With so much hype and anticipation for Earnhardt's arrival into NASCAR Winston Cup, he has already been called the "Face of NASCAR in the 21st Century." Rather than shy away from such lofty expectations, Earnhardt looks forward to fulfilling the promise.

"Hopefully, when they write that book or that magazine and they write about the 50 best drivers, 50 years from now, I'll be on that list somewhere because I hate that I missed this last one," Earnhardt says, referring to last year's 50th Anniversary celebration. "I guess I was just too young."

5

ROOKIE E

From *Stock Car Racing* magazine, July 2000,

Lessons Learned

By the end of 1999, Dale Earnhardt Jr. had won his second straight Busch Series title and was looking ahead to his inaugural Winston Cup campaign. He compiled 13 victories during his two seasons running full-time in Busch and became one of the top young drivers in NASCAR. Then it was on to bigger and better things in Winston Cup, where Earnhardt Jr. had his debut run at Charlotte in May of 1999. His best finish in five Cup races that year was a 10th at Richmond. He entered the series full-time the next year as part of one of the best rookie classes in Winston Cup history.

The 2000 Winston Cup season started with what was considered by many to be the most competitive rookie crop in at least two decades, maybe ever. Racing observers frequently compared the rookies in the class of 2000 with that of the 1979 campaign, which included seven-time Winston Cup champion Dale Earnhardt and Harry Gant.

"I think it's one of the best and most diverse as well," says NASCAR historian Bob Latford. "There's so much talent—proven talent—whether in Busch, or in CART, or wherever they came from. It's going to be a tough one and probably one of the best groups in a long time."

The list of first-year drivers includes Dale Earnhardt Jr., Matt Kenseth, Stacy Compton, Scott Pruett, Ed Berrier, Dave Blaney, Jeff Fuller, and Mike Bliss.

Shades of the late-model days and Earnhardt Jr. working on his car still flashed during the rookie campaign. *Nigel Kinrade*

A win at Texas in April came in just the seventh race of Earnhardt Jr.'s rookie season in Winston Cup. *Nigel Kinrade*

Yet, despite their experience in other series—some of it considerable and noteworthy—making the move to Winston Cup is a whole other animal.

For some, such as Earnhardt Jr. and Kenseth, it means going from the top of the Busch Series ladder to the bottom of Winston Cup. And for guys like Pruett, who laughs at the fact that he's a rookie again at 40, it means learning a new way of driving.

This year's rookies also have to follow the success of last year's rookie winner, Tony Stewart, who had the best season ever for a rookie driver, earning three victories and finishing in the top ten in points. In one season, Stewart set the bar higher for all others.

Ratcheting up the scrutiny of the rookie drivers is the arrival of Kenseth and Earnhardt on the Winston Cup Series. The two battled for the Busch Series title and their teams draw a lot of attention to the rookie race.

Living up to Stewart's record is not something Kenseth says he worries about.

"I don't think it's realistic to expect that of any of us," says Kenseth. "He had an exceptional series. I think Tony Stewart is the exception, not the norm. The best we can do is the best we can do. Every week we need to do the best we can do. If the best we can do is 13th place, fine."

Dale Jr. and the Eurys, Tony Sr. and Tony Jr., celebrated at the track that also brought their first Busch win in 1998. *Nigel Kinrade*

A pair of Winston Cup rookies, Tony Eury Jr. and Earnhardt Jr., talk things over at Pocono in June of 2000.
Nigel Kinrade

Dad checks things out before Earnhardt Jr. hits the track.
Harold Hinson

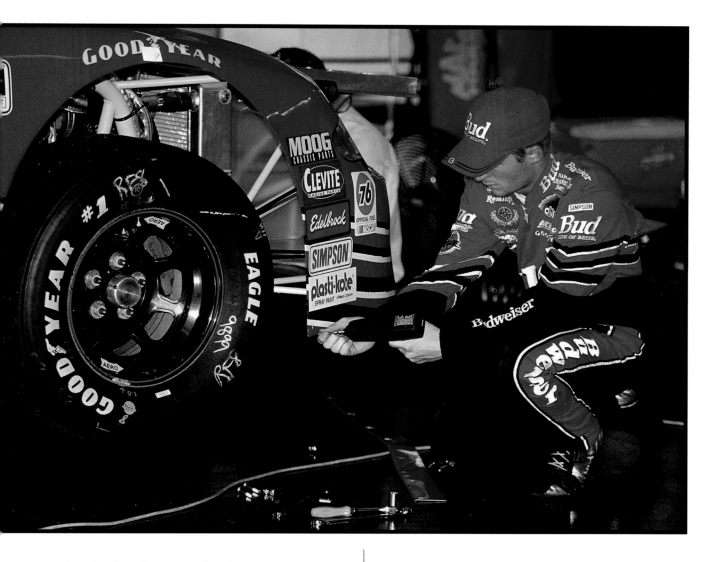

In 2000, Earnhardt Jr. was a rookie sensation in Winston Cup, and he was just three years removed from his late-model career. *Nigel Kinrade*

Earnhardt, who must also live in his father's shadow, has said repeatedly he's not going to let outside influences put more pressure on him than he's already putting on himself.

The struggle to make races only adds pressure to the already tension-filled world of being a Winston Cup driver. Yet none of them are going to let the added pressure of being rookies and the glare of the media spotlight get the best of them.

"The best thing that probably happened to me was when Gary Nelson sat down with me and told me some things that nobody else had said to me before," says Earnhardt Jr. "Even though a lot of good things have happened to me in my career, I sometimes need to be told that I'm a good race car driver. Just like being in a marriage. Even though your wife knows you love her, you've still got to tell her sometimes. That was kind of the situation I was in. It was like it'd be nice to get patted on the back sometimes even though we had a bad weekend. To hear it from somebody like Gary Nelson, who can't play favorites and to have nothing to gain by telling me that I'm going to make it, that sounds pretty good to me."

Earnhardt Jr. says he learned other lessons early in his rookie season, particularly on restrictor plate tracks. *(continued on page 87)*

THE FIRST VICTORY

At Texas Motor Speedway in 2000, Dale Earnhardt Jr. did a lot to improve the image of rookies by winning his first Winston Cup race in only the seventh event of the season.

Did he think he could win in his rookie year?

"I thought so," he said from victory lane. "I think we're going to see a couple of rookies get into victory lane this year. I didn't know how quickly it would come. I'm kind of overwhelmed with what happened today. It's just crazy, man.

"After the last three weeks, it was fun to get out front and show these guys I could use my head and make smart decisions. Even when I've got a real fast car and I'm not up front, I can be patient and pick my way through there. It was fun to prove that to them and prove my status as far as a driver goes."

Four races later, at Richmond International Raceway, Earnhardt Jr. claimed his second Winston Cup victory. His momentum continued in the tour's next event, at Lowe's Motor Speedway, as he won the pole for the Coca-Cola 600. The race, however, belonged to fellow rookie Matt Kenseth, who won for the first and only time in 2000. Kenseth also edged Earnhardt Jr. for 2000 Winston Cup Rookie of the Year.

Giving dad a love tap at Talladega. *Harold Hinson*

Elliott Sadler was fresh off a runner-up campaign to Rookie of the Year Tony Stewart when he and rookie Earnhardt Jr. talked at Daytona in February of 2000. *Nigel Kinrade*

After battling for two seasons in the Busch Series, where Earnhardt Jr. won back-to-back titles, Matt Kenseth and Earnhardt Jr. brought their friendly rivalry to Winston Cup in 2000. *Nigel Kinrade*

In Busch, Kenseth had a runner-up points finish in 1998 and a third-place effort in 1999. *Nigel Kinrade*

Kenseth gained the upper hand by edging out Earnhardt Jr. and winning Rookie of the Year in Winston Cup. *Nigel Kinrade*

Earnhardt Jr. displayed his short-track prowess with a win on Richmond's three-quarter-mile layout. *Nigel Kinrade*

(continued from page 83)

"When you first come in as a rookie, it's really hard to know when to go, when to make a run, when to attempt a pass, and when you need to stay in the draft," he says. "It was real hard for me when I first started running at Daytona and Talladega to know when to do that, and when not to, and what was a smart move.

"The whole time you're out there, especially when you're a rookie, all you're trying to do is

Rookie E sits for a studio photograph at Daytona in February. *Nigel Kinrade*

The night race at Richmond on May 6, 2000, became the scene of Earnhardt Jr.'s second win, tying him with Davey Allison for the fastest two wins in Winston Cup history. Both men won their 2nd race in their 16th attempt. *Nigel Kinrade*

impress the guys around you. You've watched Terry Labonte and Bill Elliott and all those guys race for years and all you're trying to do is to do things to impress them, to where you'll get out of the car and they'll pat you on the back. I mean, that's all you're looking for.

"So it took me awhile, took me a couple of races, a couple of years. Like in the Busch Series, I crashed out pretty much every one of the plate races I ran. And that was just because I didn't know when to be aggressive and when not to be aggressive and just kept getting myself in the wrong situations.

"Then when you come into the Cup series, you've got to know when to be in the low line and you've got to know when to be in the high line. You've got to know when changing lines is going to improve your position. It's real tough and it's hard to figure that out. I used to race as hard as I

FORGET DYNASTY—WE WANT A RIVAVLRY

BY JEFF HUNEYCUTT
From *Circle Track* magazine, October 2000

Richard Petty had David Pearson, Darrell Waltrip had Cale Yarborough, Superman had Lex Luthor. For a while, poor Jeff Gordon had nobody to keep him from rolling to double-digit victories, which made for a couple of pretty boring Winston Cup seasons. The best rivalries, of course, are the ones that are between competitors or teams battling over championships. Think Lakers versus Celtics, McEnroe versus Connors, Godzilla versus that bug thing.

On the Winston Cup side, we have the makings of a fantastic rivalry bubbling up right in front of us. Dale Earnhardt Jr. and Matt Kenseth, both Cup rookies, have already done something in the first half of the season that many veterans in the field can only dream of: They've won races. In fact, Earnhardt Jr. has already won three including The Winston. Kenseth finished an amazing sixth in his first-ever Winston Cup race in 1998. Both have the makings of future greats—and rivals.

One of the keys to growing a great rivalry is that the combatants keep bumping into each other. Earnhardt and Kenseth do seem to keep squaring off against one another. In two seasons on the Busch Series (1998–1999), Earnhardt claimed the championship, and Kenseth was his constant and greatest challenger. Although Earnhardt has claimed most of the limelight with 2 wins after 14 races, he didn't lead the rookie standings thanks to Kenseth's steady string of solid finishes.

Interestingly, despite their battles on the track, there is no animosity between the two. In fact, they are honestly friends. When Kenseth won his first Cup race in the Coca-Cola 600, Earnhardt—who had dominated the early stages—was one of the first to congratulate him. Both respect the other as a driver although their styles differ greatly. Kenseth is as cool as a cucumber, while Earnhardt is a hard driver who seems to have inherited his competitive fire from his daddy, seven-time Winston Cup champ Dale Earnhardt Sr. So here's to hoping that in the not-so-distant future, one of these young men will be challenging for his first championship, and the other will be right there, trying to take it away.

The Earnhardts were tight at Daytona for the season-opening IROC race in 2000.
Kevin Thorne

could and never get anywhere, almost lose three or four spots. And my dad could whip right up through there, no problem. I would be like, 'Man, how come I keep getting in the wrong line and he seems to keep getting in the right line?' And you just kind of figure that out. There's no way to really tell you, 'All right, this is how you do it to get to the front.' You just have to be sitting there in the car when the time comes to know, 'All right, this line is getting ready to move forward three or four lanes. I'm getting in it.' You hop in it and pick up three or four spots and get back to the bottom line and make a few moves there. And you do it without really being aggressive. You hope that when you're done, you're up front and everybody wonders how you got there, you know? That way you haven't caused too much trouble doing it."

Earnhardt Jr. earned a spot in the IROC Series by winning the Busch championship. *Paul Melhado*

6

ORDINARY GUY, EXTRAORDINARY LIFE

BY THOMAS POPE
From *Stock Car Racing* magazine, January 2001

Trying to Remain a Regular Joe

As Dale Earnhardt Jr. tackled the challenges of being a Winston Cup star, he had every reason to become a changed person, intent on living the celebrity life and counting the money that was piling up. Much of the same Earnhardt Jr. remained, however, from the guy who ran late-models and hung out with the guys at Myrtle Beach. Through the whirlwind of attention and high expectations that came from being the son of Dale Earnhardt, "Little E" was striving to be himself.

Dale Earnhardt Jr. is, in business parlance, multi-tasking. He's just stepped back into his Mooresville, North Carolina, home after paying a visit to Dale Earnhardt, Inc. There are four race shops there, totaling 200,000 square feet, but he's been to the biggest—the sparkling, sprawling main facility accurately christened the "Garage Mahal" by Darrell Waltrip. It's all just minutes from Dale Earnhardt Jr.'s house, which is located on the same 350-acre site. His father, the seven-time NASCAR Winston Cup champion in pursuit of an eighth, had summoned him over to take part in a press conference where it was announced that Dale Jr. and Steve Park will have another Cup teammate in 2001: Michael Waltrip.

The announcements made, the interviews out of the way, and the photos snapped, Earnhardt Jr. has made the short trip back to his sanctuary, pecking away on one of the four computers in his house. He's chatting long-distance to yet another reporter, and doing so without missing a beat while simultaneously checking his email and surfing the Internet. He's liable to run across an audio file he'll download and burn onto a CD, and it could be anything across the musical landscape—from Joe Cocker to Rush to Neil Young.

Dale Earnhardt Jr., despite millions pouring in from all angles, has tried to remain a regular Joe and he keeps his racing career as his top priority. Earnhardt Jr. says the trick to staying that way is to remember where you came from. *Harold Hinson*

Despite enjoying a phenomenal year, including 2 wins in his first 16 races, Earnhardt Jr.'s first full season in Winston Cup had the usual rookie mishaps. *Harold Hinson*

Diamond to Elvis

In other words, he's just being 25-year-old Dale Earnhardt Jr., the hottest commodity in NASCAR racing for most of the last three years. At least one day a week, publicist Jade Gurss tries to keep Earnhardt Jr.'s schedule free of interviews. As willingly accommodating as Earnhardt Jr. is, six days a week of the same type of questions—"If you and your dad are racing for the win on the last lap, would you wreck him?"—is about all he can stand.

"I don't mind that much. I look at every interview as a chance to improve my speaking skills and learn what's tasteful and distasteful," he says. "There have been some things I've said and shouldn't have said. Everybody has to learn the ropes.

"Like the press conference today. I basically went over to show people I'm down with my father hiring Michael to run this third Winston Cup car. I know I must've gotten interviewed five or six times, and in every one of them somebody asked me, 'What do you think about Michael?' I don't want to give people the same answer over and over, so I looked at it as a challenge and tried to answer it differently every time and speak intelligently about it. I love doing stuff like that."

A Star Is Born

At the age of 17, Dale Earnhardt Jr. began his racing career by driving street stocks around Concord (North Carolina) Motorsport Park. Eight years later, he is a two-time champion of NASCAR's Busch Series; the winner of two Winston Cup races in his rookie season, as well as NASCAR's all-star race, The Winston; and has earned more than $5 million on the track in the past three seasons.

He's the adopted favorite of his father's fans and will surely inherit their full loyalty when "Big E" puts his driving career in park sometime this decade. Yet there's no shortage of fans who pepper the stands clad in the rich red colors of the number 8 Budweiser Chevrolet.

He's handling it—the on- and off-track expectations—with a maturity that is rare among 25-year-olds.

Earnhardt Jr. is gifted with his father's skill behind the wheel, including a win-or-wreck-trying attitude. *Nigel Kinrade*

"He surprised a lot of people, including me," Dale Earnhardt says. "We knew he could drive a race car, but until you start winning on the racetrack and see how you react to the daily pressure, it's hard to know what you've got inside you."

"You can harness pressure, and sometimes it can be your enemy. You've got to use it as a positive," Dale Jr. says. "When you go back to the house or the motorcoach, that's the time to forget about it. You've got to be strong with it.

"This year has been easier than two years in Busch [where] I stepped into a car that had won. If I was going to prove myself, it was going to be in that car. If I didn't win, I was a schmuck. This is a new team. So maybe we've got some excuses, if you will. Budweiser has been very good to me, giving me days off. I have a lot of time to myself. I don't want to get burned out. I want to stay in this sport for a while."

Based on the lessons he's learned as a Winston Cup rookie, he's on the right track.

The Winston Cup Road

As a whole, Winston Cup racing hasn't been very intimidating to the son of The Intimidator. It wasn't intimidating last year, either, when he and Budweiser scheduled five chances to make Cup races. He batted a thousand, making all five races in first-round qualifying and posting a top ten finish—a sixth—in Richmond, Virginia.

Although he isn't a big spender, "Little E" is determined to enjoy his good fortune and not let his growing wealth go to his head. *Sam Sharpe*

Earnhardt Jr.'s best runs early in 2001 came on the 1- to 1.5-mile tracks. *Paul Melhado*

He carried that qualifying momentum over into 2000, grabbing a top-ten starting spot in six of the first seven races, including a front-row berth at the 1.54-mile Atlanta Motor Speedway. The first six events of the season produced mixed results: a top ten and two top twenties, followed by three straight runs of 29th place or worse.

There were a few bumps and bruises along the way as Earnhardt Jr. trudged through the second half of his inaugural Winston Cup campaign. *Nigel Kinrade*

Race number 7 hit the racing world like a sledgehammer. Nine days after Steve Park gave Dale Earnhardt, Inc. its first Winston Cup pole position, Dale Earnhardt Jr. brought home the organization's first victory.

At Texas Motor Speedway, another high-banked 1.5-miler, Dale Earnhardt Jr. simply stomped the stuffing out of the best stock car drivers in the world. He led more of the DIRECTV 500 than anyone else, blitzing to victory lane on the same piece of Fort Worth real estate where he scored his initial Busch victory just two years earlier.

Crew chief Tony Eury and chassis specialist Tony Eury Jr. "built a good car, and I pretty much did what I wanted in the car," Earnhardt Jr. says. "It did what I asked it to do. We didn't change anything all day. When we got a set of tires, I just adjusted my driving to them. I'd just point and shoot, and that thing went.

"On the last lap, I was so excited, and I could see the fans getting excited. When I turned through Turn 4, I saw all the flashbulbs flashing. I couldn't believe it—people screaming and cheering. I couldn't believe it."

The suds had barely stopped flowing at "Club E," the romper room in the basement of his home, when he had reason to celebrate again. Four weeks later, at Richmond (Virginia) International

Earnhardt Jr. realized he stepped onto a stage unlike
any other when he made the move up to Winston Cup.
Nigel Kinrade

Fans swarm whenever Earnhardt Jr. shows up. *Nigel Kinrade*

Raceway, Earnhardt beat on Tony Stewart going down pit road, and then beat everybody else to the checkered flag. The collision on pit row left Stewart with a flat tire and raised hackles, but Earnhardt insisted he had no other course of action.

"I would have been pretty happy to finish second behind Tony," Earnhardt Jr. says. "Then we had the caution, and Tony kind of made it tight coming out of the pits, and I did all I could to keep from running over the boys in [Geoffrey Bodine's pits]. The guy who was changing the right rear tire on [Bodine's] car was jumping out of my way. I couldn't have gotten any closer without hitting that car.

"It was just a bad situation. Tony was coming out of the pits behind us, so he couldn't just make a hard right and left and come out of the pits. He came straight out of his box. I guess he just didn't anticipate me coming out at about the same time.

"The pit-road deal could have easily torn my tire up. I was lucky and fortunate it didn't, but it did tear up the fender bad to where the car didn't handle the same as it was. We were still good enough and had new tires where we could hang on there. We had a pretty decent lead. I don't think if I hadn't been able to get by my dad and get that lead we had that we'd have won the race. Terry [Labonte] and them were pretty strong there at the end."

"The autograph thing can be difficult. If you go somewhere there are, say, 600 people, it's a lot more fun because you can spend a little extra time with each fan," said Dale Earnhardt Jr. *Harold Hinson*

Sixteen career starts with two wins is a feat only Davey Allison had also accomplished. But the spring rampage wasn't over yet. The Texas victory earned Earnhardt Jr. a place in The Winston, held at the high-banked, 1.5-mile Lowe's Motor Speedway. And just as he had done at Texas, Earnhardt Jr. almost toyed with the competition, becoming the first rookie to win the all-star event.

Four nights later, he returned to the same track to capture the pole position for the Coca-Cola 600. He hammered the field again, leading the most laps, but in the end, the car didn't handle as well as it had earlier in the night. As Earnhardt Jr. coasted back to the garage

Earnhardt Jr. managed some downtime at Dover in June of 2000—a rarity for the hottest rookie ever in NASCAR. *Nigel Kinrade*

There's no mistaking that Earnhardt Jr. has his own distinctive style, which is one more reason fans identify with him. *Harold Hinson*

area with a solid fourth-place finish, another rookie—Earnhardt Jr.'s good buddy, Matt Kenseth—rolled into victory lane.

In less than three months, Dale Earnhardt Jr. had more than lived up to the incredibly high expectations heaped on him. "I kind of blew 'em off there at the start of the year and didn't think much about it," he says of dealing with others' expectations. "We knew we had excuses to fall back on if we didn't run well because we were a rookie team. I mean, we had won two Busch Series

Earnhardt Jr. led the way at Michigan. *Nigel Kinrade*

Despite starting from the pole, Earnhardt Jr. finished 31st at Michigan on August 20, 2000, but he still looked very much like the son of The Intimidator. *Nigel Kinrade*

championships, but this was a completely different deal. We were all pretty much new to Winston Cup racing. The cars are different, and the engines make a bunch more horsepower. It's tougher to get the car balanced just right. So we had our excuses ready. Then we won a couple of races and I was thinking, 'This is cool. We're one of the teams to be reckoned with.'"

The Slump

Then came the summertime blues.

The Budweiser Chevys weren't bad, but they and their driver weren't running up front anymore. Earnhardt Jr. didn't lead a single lap for two full months, from mid-June until mid-August, when he won the pole position at Michigan Speedway and led 13 early circuits before winding up 31st, a lap down. The road courses—Sears Point Raceway in northern California and Watkins Glen International in upstate New York—proved particularly troublesome. Earnhardt Jr. tested at Sears Point and took several off-track detours trying to get the hang of its corners, and finished a middling 24th when the circuit went there to race a month later. At Watkins Glen, he tore up his primary car in practice and crumpled the backup in the race.

"We were all disappointed," he says. "We changed some personnel around, and we put pressure on ourselves to get back to victory lane.

"When I ran late-models, I didn't win much, but I didn't care—it was just a hobby. I was just having fun traveling up and down the road, and my buddies and I were all together. Then when I started Busch racing, my thought was, 'It's time to get serious. Losing won't be accepted.' But I really didn't have to deal with the downtimes then because we were winning races and championships, and we were always the focus. You know, everybody's saying it's one of the best things to happen in the Busch Series in a long time, [the rivalry between] Matt and me. TV ratings for the Busch Series were up.

"We moved to Winston Cup and thought we could do it, and we were all excited about it. It's weird how some of this stuff has turned out. We ran decent, but we struggled

At Pocono, Earnhardt Jr. and Dale Jarrett chat during driver introductions. *Nigel Kinrade*

at Rockingham and Darlington at the beginning of the year like I thought we would. Well, we went back to Darlington for the Southern 500, ready to fail, but did well and finished 11th. We tested at Martinsville in the spring and were really happy with the car, then went back and ran like crap, even though we did have battery problems. At Richmond, we win in May, then go back and test for the fall race since we were in the No Bull 5 deal, and we got the car even better in the test than when we had won there. We go back for the race and had a different right-side tire than we had tested with, that kind of threw our setup off, and we struggled in the race. I'm thinking, 'Damn, what the hell? We can't get the car to turn.'

"Things like that happening every four out of five weeks make you realize how tough a climb up the hill it is in Winston Cup racing."

That, perhaps, has been his biggest adjustment: realizing that he's not always going to have the best car, week in and week out. The Eurys are also learning about how to make magic with Winston Cup cars, but they don't accept any excuses.

"They feel very responsible for that car, even when there's nothing they could have done to keep mechanical stuff from going wrong," Earnhardt Jr. says. "When the battery goes dead, my re-action is to say, 'We would've had a great run if not for that battery.' They don't react like that. They get all pissed off, and that sends a message to the rest of the team about the fire and determination it takes to be successful in Winston Cup racing. When Tony Sr. gets that attitude, the guys

Under the watchful eye of Dad at Talladega during his rookie season, Earnhardt Jr. gave Rusty Wallace a friendly nudge. *Nigel Kinrade*

on the team know they're either with him or they go home. He's like Bobby Knight without the grabbing and cussing. He knows how to get his point across even though he's not an easy guy to approach. He's a very good motivator.

"We don't need a lot of motivation, though. When we won the first Busch championship, the motivation the next year was to do it again and prove that it wasn't a fluke. Then our motivation when we moved to Winston Cup was to be the first Busch team that's moved up to Cup and done well. Now our motivation is for people who don't think we're serious, to prove them wrong. But I don't have to rely on Tony or Tony Jr. to fire me up if I get slack. I search for things to motivate me. I get easily psyched."

Dale Earnhardt Jr.'s job doesn't begin and end with the race car. He's been heavily involved in marketing programs for Budweiser, but not more than he's comfortable handling. And then there is the ongoing, everyday business of dealing with fans.

Although earning the pole for the May race at Charlotte in 2000, Earnhardt Jr. finished fourth as fellow rookie Matt Kenseth grabbed his first Winston Cup victory. *Nigel Kinrade*

The Other Side of Life

In Mooresville, he says, he can still maintain some semblance of a normal life. It is, he notes, "Race City, U.S.A.," the home to more NASCAR teams than anyplace else, and fans aren't as fazed by a driver's presence in their midst. If he needs to stock up on groceries, toilet paper, or more Bud, he can do his own shopping without too many interruptions.

"Ninety-nine percent of the fans are great, but that other one percent—man, I don't know," he says. "There's always that one who's had too much to drink or wants to talk about his wife and how bad she wants to have sex with me. That's weird, man—my mind ain't wanting to try to understand that. Or the girl who wants you to sign her panties—that embarrasses me in public.

"And I go to races or an appearance someplace, and some of these fans have bags full of stuff they want me to sign. Where's it going? I'm hoping it's for family or friends, but there are two or three every weekend that are taking that stuff and selling it on eBay, and that's just not right.

"The autograph thing can be difficult. If you go somewhere there are, say, 600 people, it's a lot more fun because you can spend a little extra time with each fan. Like, 'Where'd you get this car?' Or, 'Boy, this is a nice diecast,'" he says. "When you do 2,000 people, you can't spend that kind of time with the fans because you can only sign 1,000, and you leave 1,000 pissed. You've got to hurry up. Of the 1,000 you sign, the guy in front's pissed because you ran him off, the one at the end of the line is happy because he got his autograph, and the ones in the middle don't know what to think because they got herded through like cattle. It's a hard situation—you definitely can't make everyone happy, but I try to do the right thing at the time."

And then there's the money—lots of it. Until his racing career took off, he figured he'd spend a good chunk of his life as a mechanic at Dale Earnhardt Chevrolet in Newton, North Carolina. He was doing that for $200 a week when he raced late-model stock cars and won only 3 times in 112 starts. Now that he can afford anything his heart desires, he describes himself as a relative tightwad, considering his net worth.

He's bought some cars—a 1969 Camaro, a 1971 Corvette, and a 1996 Impala that's loaded down with an earth-shattering audio system—and a pickup truck. He's got his house, a 25-foot

Earnhardt Jr. peered into his father's Chevrolet at Rockingham in October of 2000. *Nigel Kinrade*

boat, his computers built primarily for video gaming, and "Club E." The rest of it?

At Charlotte for the running of The Winston in 2000, Earnhardt Jr. rode alone during pre-race ceremonies.
Nigel Kinrade

"Of the money I've made since the beginning of 1998, I've still got 90 percent of it, if not more than that," he says. "Most of it is in stocks and money market funds. My dad introduced me to the right people, and they said, 'This is what you need to do.'

"When I was driving late-model stocks, I knew my dad was doing really well financially, and I started thinking, 'What if I do well? I want to be smart. I don't want to be broke at 50,'" he says.

"Let me tell you a story about that—about how I am with my money. When I was racing at Myrtle Beach, I started dating this girl down there, and everybody down there was driving big Chevy pickups, and I've got this little red S-10 pickup. I'm figuring if I'm going to impress her, I've got to have one of those like everybody else does.

"Well, I took the truck down to the dealer to have some brake work done, and I saw this big Chevy. Remember, I'm paying $100 a month for my truck, and the dealership's paying me $200 a week, but I went out and bought this big ol' truck, and I'm stuck with a $340-a-month payment. I drove that truck for about three months and realized, 'Man, this is too expensive. I don't give a damn whether this girl likes it or not—she's got to like me for me. I can't afford this.' I sold that truck for $16,000, paid off the $14,000 I owed on it, and bought a 1986 S-10 that was six years older than the one I had had to begin with. I drove that thing for four years and saved every dime I had."

The Intimidator's son became the first rookie to win The Winston, NASCAR's annual all-star event. *Kevin Thorne*

Earnhardt Jr. celebrated The Winston win in Charlotte's victory lane with Dad. *Harold Hinson*

The Earnhardts stand with other drivers included in the R.J. Reynolds bonus program at Talladega in April of 2000.
Nigel Kinrade

Solving the complexities of Winston Cup racing are far more difficult than being fiscally responsible. But it's obvious only one year into Dale Earnhardt Jr.'s career that the pieces are all in place for a long, successful career—one that may have the components to match the best father-son team NASCAR has ever seen, Lee and Richard Petty. Earnhardt Jr. has youth on his side as well as his father's guts. He's got an eight-figure sponsorship to pay for the best equipment money can buy or build, and proven champions in the Eurys in his corner. As for himself, the challenges he's handled—dealing with success as well as defeat—prove that Dale Earnhardt Jr. not only has his feet on the ground, but also has his head screwed on straight. That's multi-tasking for you.

7

BEHIND THE WHEEL

BY DALE EARNHARDT JR.
From *Stock Car Racing* magazine, September 2001

Dale Jr. Writes About His Experiences
Behind the Wheel of the Budweiser Chevrolet

It started out as a simple question at a midweek press conference prior to the 2001 Coca-Cola 600 at Lowe's Motor Speedway. "What do you see and feel out there?" a reporter asked Dale Earnhardt Jr. The question and Little E's subsequent answer clicked with David Bourne, editor of *Stock Car Racing*. Later, at Bourne's request, Earnhardt Jr. agreed to pen a cover story for the magazine.

Junior took us inside the cockpit of his number 8 Budweiser Chevrolet, offering rare insight into a 200-mile-per-hour sport. Racing With "E," complimented by Doug Miller's excellent portrait photography, became one of *Stock Car Racing*'s most popular stories in 2001.

Stock Car Racing magazine asked me if I could offer some of my thoughts about what it's like inside the cockpit of a Winston Cup car while we're racing for 400, 500, and even 600 miles. I'll try to describe some of the sensations and what it feels like to me.

First of all, driving a race car for a living is fun. It's fun as hell driving that fast whether we're racing or practicing. On the other hand, I'd rather not have to test so much because it's not so exciting. You're out there trying to be as much of a robot as possible so the team can make a real comparison between the changes they have made to the car. I have to be as accurate and as consistent as I can be so we can find out what works and what doesn't. It can be challenging, but most of

> By time this photograph was taken, Earnhardt Jr. was one of the most recognizable drivers in auto racing.
> *Doug Miller*

STOCK CAR RACING

STOCK CAR RACING

by DALE EARNHARDT JR.

the time during a test, I'm wondering how I could have a CD player installed in the car.

Earnhardt Jr.'s on-track success is the result of talent inherited from his father and the top-notch team that surrounds him. *Doug Miller*

Drafting

I get asked a lot about what it's like driving a car at 200 miles per hour. In some ways, it's easy. It's just simple physics. You have four tires on the car that connect to the asphalt or concrete. The key is to drive the car to the absolute edge of the tire's ability to grip that surface. It feels like you are on the verge of crashing at any moment when you're fighting a poor-handling car, but you just have to

"When I strap myself into my race car, the concentration level goes through the roof, especially at mentally draining tracks like Talladega,"—Earnhardt Jr. *Nigel Kinrade*

keep your foot in it and try to find that spot of ultimate speed.

At places like Talladega, I could teach just about anybody to go out there and run at top speed. It's so wide and the banking is so high, it's no big deal to drive at those speeds. I can have entire conversations on the radio with the team while I'm going down the endless back straight there. It seems like it's a mile long.

Now racing against 42 other cars at that speed is a different story. I don't think there is any other track that requires the concentration that Talladega does. It's not really because of the speed, but because we all run so close together with the NASCAR superspeedway aero rules. You have to be totally focused at all times when you're running cars three-wide. You almost hold your breath when you're in the middle line. You run a few laps like that and you can't believe nobody's crashed. I love it though. It's mentally challenging to run like that for three or four hours. It's like a chess match: if you get a good run, you may pass 10 cars, but you can drop back just as quickly if you are not totally focused on everything that goes on around you.

Some people said my dad could see the air coming around those cars, but I think he was able to use all of his knowledge about the air and the way to use it to pass guys. His peripheral vision was awesome—he could damn near see behind him so he was always one move ahead of the next guy.

The best way to describe the effects of the draft at Daytona or Talladega is to compare it to driving on the highway behind a big 18-wheeler. You swing your car into the passing lane to go around, and maybe for a split second the air coming off the truck makes your car feel light and jittery like it wants to be blown off the highway. Well, take that feeling and multiply your highway speed by three, and that's what it feels like all the time in the draft. The air does strange things—it sometimes feels like there's a beach ball in between you and the car in front of you as you close in. The air buffets your car and you can feel it vibrate and make your car move as you close up on his rear bumper.

"When you're running well at any track, your brain is totally focused and completely in tune with the race car and the racetrack,"—Earnhardt Jr. *Nigel Kinrade*

"Everyone on the team is focused on getting me to the front. Every crewman must be in sync during pit stops."
– Earnhardt Jr. *Harold Hinson*

"When you do it enough, it becomes almost instinctive to be going that fast."—Earnhardt Jr.
Doug Miller

On the Inside

At nearly every other track, the four contact patches of those tires are absolutely critical and that's why you hear drivers moaning or cheering about a new tire compound. If you have a winning car setup and then Goodyear changes those tire compounds, you have to start all over again.

I was vocal a couple of times last year when I complained about the consistency of the tires, but I have to say that the tires this year have been great—very consistent from set to set and track to track. You get so in tune that you can feel every part of the car and each of those four tires as they go around the track. You are strapped in the seat so tight that you feel like the car is a part of you, and the entire snarling beast is rotating just about where your ass meets the seat. When it's right, it's a great feeling.

When you're running well at any track, your brain is totally focused and completely in tune with the race car and the racetrack. However, when you're running poorly, it can be a struggle. If you crashed early and you come back out on the track, you're 100 laps down and all you are doing is logging laps, whoa—that's tough! A lot of times my mind will wander to what is on my shopping list or what home improvements I need to make. Sometimes I think about the cold beer I can drink once I get home. You're like "get this over with, NOW!" I think that's also about the only time I really notice how hot it gets in the cars. I think on a hot day, it can be up to 140 degrees (Fahrenheit) in there, but I don't really notice unless we're under a yellow flag or the car really sucks.

"You can feel every part of the car, and each of those four tires on the track,"—Earnhardt Jr. *Harold Hinson*

Concentration and focus can be especially tough at Charlotte during the Coca-Cola 600, the longest race of the year. The last 100 miles are unbelievable because you are so drained, physically and mentally. You realize your head has been just lying on the headrest for lap after lap, and your eyes get blurry and out of focus. It's a weird feeling, but you just run out of concentration and energy.

Another twist in that race is that it finishes at night. I love racing at night—especially since I seem to do better. I won at Richmond and won The Winston last year under the lights, so people tease me that because I sleep a lot, I'm better at night. The lights make the cars look so cool, and it makes 'em look faster to the fans. However, to the drivers, it seems easier to concentrate under the lights. You can see the track better because all of the outside distractions like the fans in the stands or vehicles in the infield are now in the dark. It allows you to concentrate more on the track ahead of you than be distracted by all of the other things around you.

RADIO E

BY DALE EARNHARDT JR.

In a typical race, we will make adjustments to the car on nearly every pit stop. These include altering tire pressures, adding or removing spring rubbers, and making changes to the wedge in the rear of the car.

All of the changes are intended to get us up front and in place to challenge for the lead at the end of each race. These changes are critical, so we have to talk a lot on the radio throughout each race.

Mostly I talk with Tony Eury Jr., my cousin and the team's car chief. He is in charge of deciding what changes to make to the car before and during the race. I may also speak with Tony Eury Sr. (my uncle and the team's crew chief) or other team members as well. A lot of times we talk during yellow flag periods to ease the stress and the tension. Here are some fun (and not so fun) examples of our radio chatter during some recent races.

Sometimes Tony Jr. and his dad become more like cheerleaders than anything else. Here is one of our exchanges at Texas this year.

Tony Sr.: *"Save all the gas you can here. Don't use that accelerator pedal unless you have to."*

Me: *"Awwww. Are you kidding me? Jeez."*

Tony Sr.: *"We're still figuring, but we think you can make it. The 1 [Steve Park] and the 88 [Dale Jarrett] will need to stop again [for fuel]."*

Me: *"Well, I need to know here. If I go out there and bust my ass just trying to save fuel, I'm telling ya, it ain't gonna be driver error!"*

Tony Sr.: *"We just figured it. You'll have .87 of a gallon left as you get the checkered flag."*

Tony Jr.: *"Remember, this is Texas, you'll run out after you win this thing. Go for it. You got enough."*

I talk with other members of the crew on topics like engine temperatures. Here was a conversation I had with Jeff Clark, my team's engine tuner, who wanted to know about oil and water temperatures.

Clark: *"How do the gauges look?"*

Me: *"Nice. They're silver and they all have nice little red needles."*

I also had a little fun early into this year's running of the Coca-Cola 600 at Charlotte.

Me: *"Wassup, guys?! You guys have fun tonight, all right? ... Whoa! Somebody just threw a beer bottle at the car."*

Ty Norris (team spotter): *"Yeah, NASCAR is talking about it too."*

Me: *"It musta been a Sterling Marlin fan that threw it cuz it was a damn Coors Light."*

You never know when crap will happen. Things happen that make me so mad I want to chew through the steering wheel, but it's important to try and keep a positive attitude about coming back from adversity. We ran out of fuel at Fontana, lost a lap, and yet still came back to finish third. Here's what I had to say after losing that lap.

Me: *"Excellent. Excellent. This is JUST where I wanted to be. How could you guys let the car run outta gas?"*

Tony Jr.: *"Both computers figured we could go at least two more laps on fuel. Maybe it was because you were going so much faster."*

Me: *"I've just been driving so hard, working so damn hard, and now we're at the back."*

Tony Jr.: *"This whole damn weekend has been hard for all of us. We're just gonna get it back. Let's go get 'em and not let it end this way. You just gotta have that same attitude as last week. 'Ya gotta WANT to get back up front."*

"I'm in frequent radio contact with crew chief Tony Eury Sr. and others on the team, trying to figure out what adjustments to make during pit stops."—Earnhardt Jr. *Jeff Huneycutt*

"There's nothing like the feeling you get when your car is running well,"—Earnhardt Jr. *Sam Sharpe*

What I See

People ask if I can see things like fans in the grandstands while I'm driving that fast. I really can. When you run those speeds all the time, you just get used to them and everything seems to slow down. It must be like a professional baseball player who can almost see the stitching on a baseball that's been thrown at the plate at 95 miles per hour. The best moment

"You have to be totally focused at all times when you're running cars three-wide,"—Earnhardt Jr. *Autostock, Webb*

Earnhardt Jr. has his father's knack for getting around Talladega. *Nigel Kinrade*

"I don't think there is any other track that requires the concentration that Talladega does. It's not really because of the speed, but because we all run so close together with the NASCAR superspeedway aero rules,"—Earnhardt Jr. *Nigel Kinrade*

for that was when I won my first Winston Cup race at Texas. On the last lap, I was trying to concentrate but I could see the fans going crazy, waving and yelling and taking hundreds of flash photographs.

It's the same way talking to my crew. I guess some drivers only want to talk on the radio when they're on the straightaways. It is easier to do that, but you just get accustomed to doing things like talking to the crew while you're racing around. When it gets down to the last 10 laps though, everyone shuts up and just gives me how many laps are left. I need every ounce of my focus to go into winning that race.

The Winston last year was a good example. I had to pass 10 cars in eight laps, and my car was haulin' ass. So, the spotter and the crew just let me know how many laps were left, and I was able to drive around everyone. Believe me, I could see and hear the crowd on the last lap that night!

When you do it enough, it becomes almost instinctive to be going that fast. Sometimes it is much harder to slow down and come into the pits. It's harder than it looks to hit the right pit-road speed and then judge the distance in and out of the pit stall. Every tiny portion of a second can be so critical in the pits, and then you've got your crew guys and pit-crew guys from the teams ahead and behind you on pit lane zooming out in front of you. Then, you have to stay focused on making a good exit from the pit, so believe me, it's no 15-second vacation in there.

In the end, the technology of NASCAR is pretty simple. Everyone can get the best parts for their cars, and the cars are damn near equal. What wins races and championships are the people. The ability of a driver to communicate with his team and with his crew chief and car chief is critical. I learned that last year when we were struggling, and we've been much better this year because our people are working better together. It's so important that everyone is going in the same direction. If even one person is out of sync, you have almost no chance to win. When it does all go right, the feeling of victory is unbelievable. It is like a total release of energy and joy.

It's unbelievable! I look forward to my next chance to experience that feeling again. Soon.

"Concentration and focus can be especially tough at Charlotte during the Coca-Cola 600, the longest race of the year,"—Earnhardt Jr. *Nigel Kinrade*

"The four contact patches of those tires are absolutely critical and that's why you hear all of us drivers moaning or cheering about a new tire compound,"—Earnhardt Jr. *Nigel Kinrade*

8

JUNIOR, ON THE MOVE

BY LARRY COTHREN
From *Stock Car Racing* magazine, June 2002

NASCAR's Emerging Superstar

Seeks Balance — and Victories — in His Life

In terms of clout and exposure in the marketplace, no driver in NASCAR history did as much as fast as Dale Earnhardt Jr. As the sport began to expand into territory previously outside the scope of NASCAR, it was Earnhardt Jr., more than any other driver, who was leading the way. Fame and fortune made it necessary to find harmony between his personal life and his professional life, however, as he lifted the sport on his young shoulders—while striving to perform on the track.

It's the day after Christmas and Dale Earnhardt Jr. and three friends embark on a road trip—one of those journeys you take when you're 27, wealthy, single, and anxious to kick around for a few days.

Another friend, a 21-year-old aspiring racer, is ready to make a career move by relocating from Buffalo to the Charlotte, North Carolina, area, and Junior and company head north in a red truck borrowed from Dale Earnhardt Chevrolet. They'll lend a hand to their New York buddy and live it up a little before they return to North Carolina.

"We got just past Greensboro [North Carolina] and turned off the interstate and just followed the compass from there on out, never got on another four-lane road," says Earnhardt. "It was pretty cool going through all those back roads. We went to Washington, D.C., and took our picture in front of the White House and in front of several of the monuments. We went through Gettysburg, Pennsylvania, and saw the battlefields, but it

Earnhardt Jr. and Jeff Gordon have become NASCAR's top drawing cards. *Nigel Kinrade*

Earnhardt Jr. at Daytona. *Harold Hinson*

was about two in the morning so it was kind of hard to see what was going on. We had a good time, just kind of messed around. It took us 22 hours to get up there because we were fiddling around all day and all night."

Road trips have become prized therapy for Earnhardt, mainly because they're not at all complicated. He and some buddies will simply hop into a car and drive somewhere. Usually they'll head to a place that doesn't have a local racetrack and—here's the key—where the locals don't follow racing. It's not so much what the trips offer as what they don't offer: no public appearances

A company usually gets a lot of bang for its buck as one of Earnhardt Jr.'s sponsors. *Harold Hinson*

to worry about, no strict schedules to adhere to, no one in your face all the time wanting you to do this or that or go there. "It's been more fun and beneficial for me when I do get time off to get totally away from it, to just go somewhere and get out of my element altogether," says Earnhardt.

So on the way back from Buffalo the week after Christmas, Earnhardt and his buddies detour a little west, going through Ohio. Not exactly a place to get away from racing, given the 50 or so racetracks that dot the Ohio landscape, but a diversion nonetheless.

"We stopped at a bar and spent the night and had a good time," Earnhardt says. "It was a lot of fun. It was kind of cool just to get away and be normal for a while. That was definitely a reality check to get you pumped up about the year and get you back into life."

Eye of the Storm

Taking a road trip and relaxing is one of those requisite life functions when you're suddenly the face of an entire sport and the whole world wants a piece of your time. Or when your new book, *Driver #8*, is on *The New York Times* bestseller list.

If we peep into Earnhardt's life for a glimpse of how hectic and demanding it is to always be in the public eye, then it's easy to see why something so innocent as a road trip, nothing more than an escape into a life resembling normalcy, is so valuable.

Earnhardt's sister, Kelley, and his publicist, Jade Gurss, are charged with the task of making sense and order of Earnhardt's professional life.

"It's like a big, giant jigsaw puzzle," says Gurss, who co-authored *Driver #8*. "You have a lot of pieces that are

"The pressure is on him to continue to dazzle people with his image, his youth image, but he's got to deliver on the racetrack to keep that flame burning as strong as it is."
—*Humpy Wheeler, track promoter*

Earnhardt Jr.'s on-track performance will be the ultimate gauge of his success. *Sam Sharpe*

There were glitches along the way, but Earnhardt Jr. claimed two Busch Series titles and five Winston Cup wins during his first four complete seasons in NASCAR. *Harold Hinson*

strewn all over the place and the challenge is to get them to fit in the best way possible. If he were to do all of the interviews or all of the appearances that are requested, he would be working 24 hours, 7 days a week. In the 10 days at Daytona, he did almost 95 interviews and nearly a dozen different sponsor appearances or functions, plus one massive autograph session for his new book."

This whirlwind of attention has surrounded Earnhardt since he took the Busch Series by storm and won back-to-back titles in 1998 and 1999. Since moving up to Winston Cup in 2000, when he promptly won two races and two poles, the intensity has increased as Earnhardt has almost single-handedly redefined stock car stardom, standing before people in places previously outside the NASCAR reach.

"We've been in a unique situation to go to different places and show people a little bit about NASCAR," says Earnhardt. "I might not represent the average mold for a NASCAR driver, but we were able to go to certain areas and [see] certain people throughout the country, especially toward the West Coast last year, with some of the articles and some of the networks we worked with, and showed ourselves and our sport to some interesting groups of people."

Bringing Them In

It may seem odd that Dale Earnhardt Jr., with five wins in his first two Winston Cup seasons and a driver defined more by what he hasn't done on the track than what he has done, is the guy leading the NASCAR charge into new and mostly uncharted territory. It hasn't been that

"You can't fool the public. When you dress somebody up and they do the dance, I think the public can tell the difference between somebody who's sincere and somebody who's not,"—Earnhardt Jr. *Harold Hinson*

long since he was running late-models at Myrtle Beach, South Carolina. Now he's the face of the sport. Does that sound right?

Nearly all of the sporting press, and some on the outside looking in, think so. Look around and the guy is everywhere, including on magazine covers, in profiles, and everywhere a story can be told. Not to mention his appearances on MTV and *The Tonight Show* with Jay Leno, stories in *People* and *Rolling Stone*, and an interview in *Playboy*. This is definitely not his daddy's NASCAR, and that's the whole point.

Could it be that Dale Earnhardt Jr., the man of the hour in U.S. motorsports, is just the guy to stand before an entire country and represent stock car racing? He appears to meet all of the requirements.

"There are all kinds of things that I want to do, and I know that to be able to do [them] I'll have to continue as a race car driver and be good at it,"—Earnhardt Jr. *Nigel Kinrade*

NASCAR has long been about lineage, heritage, and many of the things in society that speak family—from American-made automobiles to children hoisted high in victory lane. NASCAR remains to this day a family-run business, one born over 50 years ago in the South and raised on traditional Southern values of hard work, loyalty, and dedication. So who better to represent the sport than a third-generation driver who is the son of the man who personified the very soul of stock car racing?

If Earnhardt Jr.'s bloodline alone is not enough to justify his place in the sport, consider this: the NASCAR growth curve demanded a younger audience, some maintain, and Earnhardt Jr. has met and exceeded the demand, and that alone has set him apart from those who've gone before him.

Humpy Wheeler, the Speedway Motorsports president who is a respected observer of the sport, says the timing was right for Earnhardt to make his mark.

"I think the pop culture that they introduced him to—or he introduced them to, that's debatable there—that's the first time that has happened, and I think it signifies the broader market we have today compared to even five years ago, particularly the youth market," says Wheeler.

"A decade ago we were beginning to be concerned that our demographics were reaching up too high as far as age was concerned. But Jeff Gordon, as he started winning, began to change that. Now Gordon is 30 and along comes Earnhardt Jr. at the right time with the right kind of personality. He's bringing that youth group along. It's just extraordinary how the demographics of this whole business are changing even as we speak."

It's not just teenagers and twenty-somethings who count themselves among the Earnhardt Jr. legion, though. Watch nearly an entire grandstand rise to its feet whenever Junior turns in a hot qualifying lap or makes a charge into the lead of a race, and you'll see a cross section of fans. He can bring that young person into the NASCAR fold, but he'll also grab the loyalty of that young person's father and grandfather. Some of those fans come from his father, no doubt, but they're in the fold either way.

A media swarm usually accompanies Earnhardt Jr. at the track. *Harold Hinson*

Another factor in Junior's ascension to the top of the sport is his ability to be himself. It's an old battle cry, but it remains a relevant one: a sport built on colorful characters lacks color today. And NASCAR drivers have long been poked fun at for their willingness to walk the walk and talk the talk to appease image-conscious sponsors. Then along comes Earnhardt Jr. with his laid-back personality, dash of color, and air of genuineness.

"I've been hearing a lot of talk about representing the sport and whether I would be one of those guys to do that or not, and maybe that's why I pressure myself on wearing just normal clothes every day and being myself," says Earnhardt. "I get a lot of flack from my sponsor for not having their logo all over my back and my shoulders and my head. Walking around in a pair of Adidas is pretty cool to me, and I want people to know that's who I am. And if you don't mind that guy who represents the sport wearing Adidas and the hat backwards, then that's fine. But if you do mind, then look somewhere else.

"You can't fool the public. When you dress somebody up and they do the dance, I think the public can tell the difference between somebody who's sincere and somebody who's not. Although I'm very proud of my relationship with all my sponsors—whether it be Budweiser or Drakkar or whoever—I don't feel like it's that necessary to don their logos everywhere I go. For some reason I think we can go further just being ourselves, and I think people will be more interested in that than billboarding."

A whirlwind of attention has surrounded "Little E" since he took the Busch Series by storm and won back-to-back titles in 1998 and 1999. *Harold Hinson*

Since moving up to Winston Cup in 2000, when he promptly won two races and two poles, the intensity has increased as Earnhardt Jr. has almost single-handedly redefined stock car stardom. *Harold Hinson*

HIT MAKER

We've seen the television commercial where Junior has problems with the CD player in his race car. But what artists would he choose if he did listen to CDs while driving 180 miles per hour? Here's what he told us, listed in the order he gave them:

1. **Bob Seger Greatest Hits**
2. **Foo Fighters**
3. **Matthew Good Band**
4. **Dr. Dre**
5. **Faith Hill**

Seeking Balance

At 27 years old, Earnhardt Jr. is firmly established in the sport at the same age his father was as a rookie. Junior epitomizes NASCAR cool while his father at 27 was a throwback to the sport's rough-hewn past. Where Earnhardt Sr.'s trademark was a bushy mustache, Junior's trademark is a ball cap worn backwards. Yet there's a mellow, somewhat domesticated nature that reveals itself, despite the road trips—or rather because of the road trips and the balance they lend to his life. Last year he even shut down "Club E," the basement nightclub at his house. No, he's not married yet, although he has said a wife and a son would go a long way toward leading a full life. But there's only so much you can pack into a life like the one he's lived the last few years.

Earnhardt Jr.'s time at the track is defined by a crush of reporters, microphones, cameras, and tape recorders.
Harold Hinson

"For the most part, it's been a lot of fun," says Earnhardt. "Even the really heavy structure, when it gets to be like we're doing something every day, it's still fun. There was a point last year and the year before that, every once in a while, where you seem to kind of lose touch with your home life and your family and your friends. This year I'm going to try to be a little more related toward that end of it, to be more involved with my friends and family than I was last year and spend some more time around them and try to get what I want out of my professional life and social life. We've been so busy running around and everything over the last couple of years that it's been really hard to maintain good relationships with my family and my friends. I'll try to do a little better with that this year.

"My mother moved from Norfolk [Virginia] about a year ago. I can just drive two miles down the road and see her, and that's really great. My sister [Kelley] had Carson, my little niece,

"If he were to do all the interviews or all of the appearances that are requested, he would be working 24 hours, 7 days a week,"—Jade Gurss, Earnhardt Jr.'s publicist. *Nigel Kinrade*

For over two decades Dale Earnhardt Sr. helped raise the popularity of stock car racing. Today, his son is at the forefront of the sport. *Harold Hinson*

Earnhardt Jr. teamed with car owner Richard Childress to win the season-opening Busch race at Daytona in 2002.
Nigel Kinrade

about a year and a half ago, and that's been a lot of fun to be around her. Those things like that have made a lot of difference."

The specter of who he is and where he's going in his chosen profession is never far away, though. Ultimately, he realizes success will be gauged solely by his performance on the track. "There are all kinds of things that I want to do, and I know that to be able to do [them], I'll have to continue as a race car driver and be good at it," he says.

There are also the inevitable questions about goals and motivation that young, rich athletes face. Earnhardt fields questions about the importance of a breakout season with reference to a couple of drivers who reached the sport's pinnacle. "It's pretty important to me," he says. "I would say it's as important as it was to my father. If there's a gauge to go off of, I believe it would be just as important to me as it was to him or to Jeff Gordon or anybody else."

Wheeler has developed a theory on stardom and its place in NASCAR. During his five decades of involvement in stock car racing and from observing sports in general, he maintains that NASCAR got to where it is today by consistently having two superstars. The same formula applies to other sports, according to Wheeler. Since Dale Earnhardt Sr.'s fatal crash a year and a

Earnhardt Jr. and Teresa Earnhardt celebrated with Richard Childress and his wife, Judy, after the Daytona victory.
Nigel Kinrade

half ago, Jeff Gordon stands as the sport's only true superstar, Wheeler maintains, and Earnhardt Jr. will have to win more often to claim a spot alongside Gordon.

"In this type of racing, to really be a superstar you've got to be a prolific winner," Wheeler says. "You can act like a superstar, you can look like a superstar, and just that charisma, those elements right there, will vault you up where everybody can see you. But you can't stay there unless you win races. So the pressure is on him to continue to dazzle people with his image, his youth image, but he's got to deliver on the racetrack to keep that flame burning as strong as it is.

"If he wins two or three races a year and we have the type of parity we have now, he might just be able to keep that going and might emerge as that second superstar."

For now, Earnhardt says his spot at the top of the sport, the spot that holds superstardom, will have to wait.

"I think," says Earnhardt, "that I will establish that a little more once we win some more races and maybe get closer to winning a championship. Right now we're just kind of growing."

Yet if we look out on the NASCAR horizon, we'll spot Earnhardt Jr. He'll be easy to pick out, and not just because of his hat turned backwards. He'll be the one with the road trips to make, family to embrace, friendships to nurture, and races to win. The key to being a superstar, after all, might be the ability to live with superstardom.

The media crush around Earnhardt Jr. at the track is exceeded only by the hordes of people lined up at his souvenir trailer. *Nigel Kinrade*

MEASURING UP

BY LARRY COTHREN

"The Only Thing That Matters to Me Is Driving and Kicking Butt."

At the end of 2002, with two seasons in the Busch Series and three in Winston Cup behind him, Earnhardt Jr. had seven Cup victories, a pair of Busch titles, and a solid place in the sport his father and grandfather helped build.

Earnhardt Jr. and the Budweiser crew won the fall race at Talladega in 2001 and both races there in 2002.
Harold Hinson

Earnhardt Jr. won at Texas and Richmond during his rookie season in Winston Cup—tying Davey Allison's record with 2 wins in his first 16 races—and he became the first rookie to win The Winston, NASCAR's annual all-star race. Then he won at Daytona in 2001, less than five months after his father's death in the Daytona 500. He also won at Dover's tough 1-mile track in his second Cup season; then, from the fall of his second season through 2002, he won three straight races at Talladega Superspeedway. Finally, he made a return trip to his old Busch Series stomping grounds in 2002 and won two of the three races he entered.

Make no mistake, this third-generation driver has made a mark in stock car racing where it counts most: on the track.

In a sport increasingly marked by parity, with 18 different winners in 2002 and 19 in 2001, Earnhardt Jr.'s domination at Talladega, in particular, has helped him continue the Earnhardt legacy in the stock car world. That, he says, makes him most proud.

"It makes me feel like I'm putting in my part as far as carrying on the Earnhardt name," he says. "That's real important to me, that there's an Earnhardt out there to cheer for, doing good enough to cheer for. That makes me feel good. I just want to keep on racking up accomplishments so that when

it's all done I can sit down and say I was a good race car driver and I made my daddy proud and I made my daddy's fans proud. But again, to some people it might not be enough because of what my daddy accomplished, you know?"

Accomplishments on the track have sometimes taken a back seat to the distractions in the modern NASCAR world. Yet strip away the glamour and attention that comes with being a Winston Cup star today, and what occurs on the racetrack becomes the only true method of evaluation. You especially don't measure an Earnhardt by the number of personal appearances he makes or by the volume of endorsements he can wrangle from the marketplace. An Earnhardt is measured by his performance between green flag and checkered flag. There is no other standard.

That was established when Ralph Earnhardt laid the groundwork for the Earnhardt legacy five decades ago, becoming the gold standard by which *all* short-track racers of his day were measured. By sheer grit and determination, Dale Earnhardt took his talent and success far beyond that of a regional star in a Southern sport. His record of 7 Winston Cup titles and 76 victories measured up against any racer of his time, as he became arguably the greatest stock car racer who ever lived.

That's the stage Dale Earnhardt Jr. stepped onto when he decided to become a stock car racer. No driver before him entered the sport with as much expected of him, or with a legacy quite like the one that came with being an Earnhardt.

Talladega has become a stronghold for Earnhardt Jr.
Nigel Kinrade

An October, 2002 victory at Talladega earned Earnhardt Jr. a Winston bonus of one $1,000,000. *Harold Hinson*

Dale Earnhardt Sr. won 10 races at Talladega, and Earnhardt Jr. has continued that success. *Nigel Kinrade*

"I watched Davey Allison and Kyle Petty, watched those guys as a kid," says Earnhardt Jr., "knowing well that I was going to be under the same circumstances at some point in time, to have to weather the storm, so to speak, when you didn't live up to the expectations that everyone set for you. I know that winning seven championships or even coming close to that is a long shot for anybody. I don't care who you are, who your daddy was, what kind of car you've got, or who you race for, it's a long shot. That's a dream career for anybody. People who win those three and four championships only come along every 5 or 10 years."

Comparisons to his father's talent and success are inevitable, of course, and some see similarities to Dale Sr. in the driving style of Dale Jr. "He still opens that door," says Buddy Baker, a 15-race winner during his NASCAR driving career and a respected observer of the sport, of Earnhardt Jr. "He's one of those kids who will go for it. I think that's what everyone likes about Dale Jr. That part of his father, the apple didn't roll far from the tree, as far as stepping up when it's time to go to battle to win. I mean, he's there."

The pressure that comes with being the son of a stock car racing icon will always be there, too, regardless of what Earnhardt Jr. accomplishes on the track. The bar will forever be raised higher

"The most important thing always comes back to communication. For some reason, I've witnessed it firsthand these past couple of years and really have been concentrating on trying to get better at talking and working things out with the crew,"—Earnhardt Jr. *Nigel Kinrade*

"I've seen the good days and bad days, and you can really tell a difference when communication is not there. It has a direct effect on how you run and how things work out for you the rest of the day,"—Earnhardt Jr. *Harold Hinson*

Earnhardt Jr. has a tight bond with the Eurys. Crew chief Tony Eury Sr. is Earnhardt Jr.'s uncle and car chief Tony Eury Jr. is his first cousin. *Kevin Thorne*

Earnhardt Jr. competed in this Richard Childress–owned Busch car at Charlotte in May of 2002. *Nigel Kinrade*

and higher, but it's something he has dealt with since he began racing.

"I had more pressure on me in late-models because I couldn't produce, couldn't really win races or be dominant, or get a handful of wins at any racetrack we went to," says Earnhardt Jr. "We would run pretty good. We would run in the top five pretty much everywhere we went, but we couldn't win any races. So I felt like I was wasting my daddy's time and money doing what I was doing. It was kind of like a 'Man, this is a lot of fun. I wonder how long it's going to last' kind of deal.

"Now I don't feel quite as much pressure. I do feel that very soon, in the next couple of years, people are going to start pointing out that I'm getting close to 30, and I'm going to get a lot of pressure to step it up or whatever. Somebody might say, 'you know, it's time for him to take the next step.' I've already read some of those articles on the Internet. That's going to be like, 'Golly, let a guy live,' you know what I mean?

"I think the older I get, people are going to continue to make a story out of something. Most of it's true and some of it is just not really relevant or impor-

Earnhardt Jr. campaigned this colorful Busch Series Chevrolet at Richmond in September of 2002 and won handily. *Nigel Kinrade*

tant. I don't know if that will be pressure or not. Whenever I get on the Internet and read something that says, 'Well, he's 28 years old and it's time for him to take the next step into maturity,' that feels like pressure to me, you know?"

Despite the opinions and high standards others might establish, there is a level of comfort and confidence off the track, especially in how Earnhardt Jr. looks at his career. That contrasts sharply with the lack of confidence he suffered early in his career. "Me personally, I'm real happy with how I've done," he says. "I don't feel like, 'Darn, I didn't accomplish this.' I feel real good.

Earnhardt Jr. had two Busch Series victories in three starts during 2002. *Harold Hinson*

Earnhardt Jr. is very popular among his fellow drivers.
Harold Hinson

When I was a teenager and just starting to race the late-model series, I was really intimidated and I wasn't too impressed at all with my driving, at that point. And I didn't think that how I was running was warranting a Winston Cup career.

"Now that I'm in Winston Cup, as long as I can look back and remember my attitude when I

Bonds form between drivers during a Winston Cup tour that covers nearly 40 weekends.
Sam Sharpe

came into late-model racing, when I started driving, then I can look at my career now and say, 'Man, I really accomplished more than I anticipated.' When you're 17 years old and sitting in victory lane at a race your dad just won, you dream about winning your own race one day. You just can't imagine . . . 'Man, that's a long road to get there.'

"So yeah, I'm real happy. I've won several races, I've done some interesting things as far as races we've won, the ways we've won, the circumstances around the races. I mean, those are great accomplishments for me personally. I look forward to just continuing, but I don't want to level off, you know? I want to get better and better and better. I expect to do more, winning championships and stuff like that down the road. But right now, the first three years, I'm pretty happy with how it's going."

The Long Road
The transformation of Dale Earnhardt Jr., late-model racer, to Dale Earnhardt Jr., NASCAR's

Teammates Steve Park, Earnhardt Jr., and Michael Waltrip will forever be linked as the men who formed the first three-driver combination at Dale Earnhardt, Inc. *Nigel Kinrade*

The Budweiser Chevrolet at Indianapolis.

Harold Hinson

hottest young driver, wasn't something that just happened. Dale Earnhardt could have put all three of his children in a top Busch Series ride at any time, but he chose the only way he knew to mold talent: by letting each of his children grow and develop slowly, and by letting them learn, on their own, the same lessons he learned.

Now, at age 28, with a decade of full-time racing behind him, from late-models to Winston Cup, Earnhardt Jr. has developed a sense of what it takes to be successful in the sport.

"The thing that separates drivers nowadays, since we're all about equally as good as each other, is how you use your head, your judgment calls, your mentality, your outlook toward the season, your effort, your presence to the team, what you bring to the table as far as morale and leadership, things like that," he says.

There is the perception, nonetheless, that Earnhardt Jr., millionaire bachelor and promoter of Budweiser and wild times, is living too fast and loose to be at peak performance on the track.

"My personal opinion of him," says Bill Wilburn, crew chief for Rusty Wallace, "is when he gets his personal life to the point where he is 100 percent focused on driving the race car and that's

The red number 8 Chevrolet is one of the most popular cars in Winston Cup. *Sam Sharpe*

all that matters in his life, I don't see him being much different than his old man, because he's shown flashes of brilliance on every kind of track there is out there. The only place I haven't seen him really flash big is on a road course, and I'm sure that's coming. It's just a matter of time.

"I'm not knocking his personal life because the kid can do whatever he wants. He's a young man and he's got the world by the tail. He's a twenty-something, single millionaire and everything in the world is at his disposal. Hey, who wouldn't take advantage of the circumstances and

Carrying on the Earnhardt legacy is important to Earnhardt Jr. *Harold Hinson*

situations that come his way? The biggest thing, though, is when he gets that stuff where he wants it and gets his mind made up to go racing 100 percent—where that's all he thinks and lives and dreams and eats—it's going to be tough to handle him. Period."

Earnhardt Jr. is aware that many observers, both inside and outside the sport, look at his personal life and perceive a lack of dedication toward becoming the best driver he can possibly be.

"I would say two years ago that was right," he says. "Two years ago I didn't understand the commitment. I didn't understand how determined and how driven you have to be. Devoted, I

The Budweiser Chevrolet is often among the fastest cars during qualifying runs.
Harold Hinson

A road course victory is one of the remaining milestones for Earnhardt Jr.
Nigel Kinrade

A pole run at Kansas City was one of two in 2002.
Nigel Kinrade

guess, would be a good word. I wanted to have fun. Driving race cars was fun. If you look back at the 1960s and 1970s, there were drivers out there who raced hard on and off the track, and I think I'm probably no different.

"These days everything benches on 12 guys in a boardroom, and I think a lot of people have forgotten what racers were like 20, 30 years ago. I'm pretty tame compared to how they were back then. Now is a different time as far as how devoted and how determined and how much time you have to dedicate to the sport to be a good driver.

"I think when I first started in my rookie season in Winston Cup, I didn't understand the commitment, and it was just because it was new. Winston Cup and Busch are two different things. In Busch, you race like hell on Saturday and on Sunday you hit the lake and meet everybody and talk about it. It was fun, and there wasn't a lot of repercussions and restrictions. In the Winston Cup Series, man, it's just cookie-cutter. You've got to be by the book. Don't step out of line.

The July 2001 victory at Daytona came just five months after the death of his father at the track. It was a triumphant event for Earnhardt Jr., DEI, and NASCAR. *Nigel Kinrade*

Look the hell out. That's kind of the deal now.

"I've gotten better this past year. You build up this reputation and I think it's really hard to dismantle it in the matter of a year. But I'm living quite the different lifestyle than I did two years ago."

One of his more notorious playgrounds was in the basement of his house, which he converted into a full-fledged private nightclub with a bar and dance floor. However, "Club E" was shut down in 2001.

"I put a pool table down there and I go down and play a little pool with three or four of my buddies," he says. "We don't have the old club we used to have. I remodeled my house, and as far as taking better care of it and as far as who comes in and who comes out, it's a little more strict. I don't have any visitors. I used to have people come over all the time, on Wednesday nights, on Sunday nights after the race. We used to gather up a group of 10 or 15 or so and just raise hell. I haven't done that in a long, long time it seems like.

"I remodeled my house, got some nice shrubbery up front, got my shop going in the back and everything. Bought some land, been working on my land. Done a lot of growing up in the last two years."

A Bit of Maturity

The Budweiser crew helped Earnhardt Jr. to an 11th-place points finish in 2002. *Harold Hinson*

With seemingly the whole world watching over the past three seasons, particularly the last two since his father died, Earnhardt Jr. has faced the demands and challenges

of being a superstar. He has, clearly, learned the lessons outside the track his father sought to instill in him. When Earnhardt Jr. says he has matured, many who know him agree. Ernie Hammonds, the self-described

Over the past two years, Earnhardt Jr. has worked to change his reputation for fast living. *Nigel Kinrade*

"general flunky" from the Myrtle Beach days, says Earnhardt Jr. has matured quite well from the shy teenager who signed autographs for 50 people without ever raising his head.

"I was at an autograph session in Bristol [Tennessee], downtown on State Street, in August [2002]," says Hammonds, "and to each and every person who went through that line he said, 'Thank you very much. Have a good day.' *To each and every one that went through that line*. So he's come a long, long way. As a *person*.

"He had every opportunity in the world to act like a couple of the other drivers have acted, and probably every reason in the world to be a jerk, and hasn't been. He's changed some, but I

Earnhardt Jr. has become a fixture in the sport while driving for the team his father built. *Nigel Kinrade*

In five years, Earnhardt Jr. has become one of the most recognizable figures in NASCAR. *Kevin Thorne*

don't think it's fair for people to say his head has gotten big since he did this. If I had somebody poking at me every 30 seconds, I would probably be that way, and I wouldn't be as nice as he is."

Yet, through the grind of being constantly in the spotlight and being pulled in several different directions, there is a yearning for simpler times, says Earnhardt Jr.

"I miss going down to Myrtle Beach, taking a couple of checks, one for tires and one for pit passes," he says, "and having a great time, you know? These days you don't know whether you're coming or going or who you're getting ready to meet. You're meeting people. 'Hey, I'm going to introduce you to this guy. I'm going to introduce you to this guy.' And you're remembering their

Earnhardt Jr. uses the same number 8 that his grandfather, Ralph Earnhardt, used while winning hundreds of short-track races in the Carolinas. *Nigel Kinrade*

Earnhardt Jr. and teammate Michael Waltrip chat during the 2002 season. *Harold Hinson*

name and face, not because the meeting was interesting and you enjoyed their company, but because you don't know whether you're going to run into them down the road and you've got to remember who they were. You know what I mean? Everything is kind of not for the right reasons anymore.

"When I get in the car, that's the best time I can get in there, and I'm doing that because I like it. That's why I've always done it, but everything kind of changed. In a matter of two years, my outlook toward things has changed dramatically. It's amazing. I can't imagine what it's going to be like five years from now."

Has he changed in two years because of the death of his father?

"I don't know if that was a cornerstone or anything, but I used to get really, really nervous about talking in front of a big crowd," he says. "Now it's a breeze, because there are so many other things out there that are tougher and harder that you'll go through, and that's nothing. I don't know whether it's because I've gotten better at it or I just don't really care anymore about it. The only thing that matters to me is driving and kicking butt and being The Man out there."

The Budweiser Chevrolet has become a force to be reckoned with in the Winston Cup Series. *Nigel Kinrade*

DALE EARNHARDT JR.'S NASCAR APPEARANCES
WINSTON CUP (1999–2002)

Year	Race No.	Race	Finish	Start	Car	Laps	Condition	Winnings
2002	1	Daytona – Daytona 500	29	5	No. 8 Budweiser Chevrolet	171	Running	$175,137
	2	Rockingham – Subway 400	26	29	No. 8 Budweiser Chevrolet	391	Running	77,587
	3	Las Vegas – UAW-DaimlerChrysler 400	16	35	No. 8 Budweiser Chevrolet	267	Running	84,875
	4	Atlanta – MBNA America 500	2	3	No. 8 Budweiser Chevrolet	325	Running	104,600
	5	Darlington – Carolina Dodge Dealers 400	4	23	No. 8 Budweiser Chevrolet	293	Running	96,542
	6	Bristol – Food City 500	4	23	No. 8 Budweiser Chevrolet	500	Running	87,850
	7	Texas – Samsung/RadioShack 500	42	9	No. 8 Budweiser Chevrolet	192	Accident	85,722
	8	Martinsville – Virginia 500	5	3	No. 8 Budweiser Chevrolet	500	Running	88,862
	9	Talladega – Aaron's 499	1	4	No. 8 Budweiser Chevrolet	188	Running	184,830
	10	California – NAPA Auto Parts 500	36	9	No. 8 Budweiser Chevrolet	225	Accident	89,987
	11	Richmond – Pontiac Excitement 400	36	2	No. 8 Budweiser Chevrolet	327	Running	76,862
	12	Charlotte – Coca-Cola 600	35	6	No. 8 Budweiser Chevrolet	371	Engine	76,575
	13	Dover – MBNA Platinum 400	30	30	No. 8 Budweiser Chevrolet	396	Running	87,492
	14	Pocono – Pocono 500	12	14	No. 8 Budweiser Chevrolet	200	Running	78,612
	15	Michigan – Sirius Satellite Radio 400	22	3	No. 8 Budweiser Chevrolet	199	Running	80,677
	16	Sears Point – Dodge/Save Mart 350	30	23	No. 8 Budweiser Chevrolet	109	Running	84,607
	17	Daytona – Pepsi 400	6	9	No. 8 Budweiser Chevrolet	160	Running	105,537
	18	Chicagoland – Tropicana 400	10	9	No. 8 Budweiser Chevrolet	267	Running	102,437
	19	New Hampshire – New England 300	23	28	No. 8 Budweiser Chevrolet	300	Running	64,925
	20	Pocono – Pennsylvania 500	37	11	No. 8 Budweiser Chevrolet	144	Running	55,100
	21	Indianapolis – Brickyard 400	22	3	No. 8 Budweiser Chevrolet	160	Running	125,280
	22	Watkins Glen – Sirius Satellite Radio at The Glen	35	21	No. 8 Budweiser Chevrolet	84	Running	57,605
	23	Michigan – Pepsi 400	10	1	No. 8 Budweiser Chevrolet	200	Running	78,740
	24	Bristol – Sharpie 500	3	2	No. 8 Budweiser Chevrolet	500	Running	131,090
	25	Darlington – Mountain Dew Southern 500	16	15	No. 8 Budweiser Chevrolet	367	Running	67,185
	26	Richmond – Chevy Monte Carlo 400	4	24	No. 8 Budweiser Chevrolet	400	Running	87,205
	27	New Hampshire – New Hampshire 300	11	37	No. 8 Budweiser Chevrolet	207	Running	70,425
	28	Dover – MBNA All-American Heroes 400	24	3	No. 8 Budweiser Chevrolet	396	Running	66,240
	29	Kansas – Protection One 400	6	1	No. 8 Budweiser Chevrolet	267	Running	96,700

Year	Race No.	Race	Finish	Start	Car	Laps	Condition	Winnings
	30	Talladega — EA Sports 500	1	13	No. 8 Budweiser Chevrolet	188	Running	$166,040
	31	Charlotte — UAW-GM Quality 500	9	13	No. 8 Budweiser Chevrolet	334	Running	69,300
	32	Martinsville — Old Dominion 500	4	10	No. 8 Budweiser Chevrolet	500	Running	75,870
	33	Atlanta — NAPA 500	5	13	No. 8 Budweiser Chevrolet	248	Running	97,950
	34	Rockingham — Pop Secret 400	34	22	No. 8 Budweiser Chevrolet	389	Running	59,100
	35	Phoenix — Checker Auto Parts 500	5	3	No. 8 Budweiser Chevrolet	312	Running	97,850
	36	Homestead — Ford 400	21	2	No. 8 Budweiser Chevrolet	267	Running	60,825
2001	1	Daytona — Daytona 500	2	6	No. 8 Budweiser Chevrolet	200	Running	975,907
	2	Rockingham — Dura Lube 400	43	25	No. 8 Budweiser Chevrolet	0	Accident	66,924
	3	Las Vegas — UAW-DaimlerChrysler 400	23	32	No. 8 Budweiser Chevrolet	266	Running	90,398
	4	Atlanta — Cracker Barrel 500	15	17	No. 8 Budweiser Chevrolet	324	Running	73,723
	5	Darlington — Carolina Dodge Dealers 400	34	16	No. 8 Budweiser Chevrolet	285	Running	64,138
	6	Bristol — Food City 500	31	9	No. 8 Budweiser Chevrolet	456	Running	77,288
	7	Texas — Harrah's 500	8	1	No. 8 Budweiser Chevrolet	334	Running	133,573
	8	Martinsville — Virginia 500	11	10	No. 8 Budweiser Chevrolet	500	Running	71,233
	9	Talladega — Talladega 500	8	19	No. 8 Budweiser Chevrolet	188	Running	90,178
	10	California — NAPA Auto Parts 500	3	38	No. 8 Budweiser Chevrolet	250	Running	136,873
	11	Richmond — Pontiac Excitement 400	7	14	No. 8 Budweiser Chevrolet	400	Running	75,348
	12	Charlotte — Coca-Cola 600	25	19	No. 8 Budweiser Chevrolet	398	Running	85,778
	13	Dover — MBNA Platinum 400	3	11	No. 8 Budweiser Chevrolet	400	Running	113,648
	14	Michigan — Kmart 400	39	7	No. 8 Budweiser Chevrolet	171	Engine	69,593
	15	Pocono — Pocono 500	20	6	No. 8 Budweiser Chevrolet	199	Running	73,288
	16	Sears Point — Dodge/Save Mart 350	19	37	No. 8 Budweiser Chevrolet	112	Running	75,718
	17	Daytona — Pepsi 400	1	13	No. 8 Budweiser Chevrolet	160	Running	185,873
	18	Chicagoland — Tropicana 400	11	36	No. 8 Budweiser Chevrolet	267	Running	70,800
	19	New Hampshire — New England 300	9	29	No. 8 Budweiser Chevrolet	300	Running	78,473
	20	Pocono — Pennsylvania 500	2	12	No. 8 Budweiser Chevrolet	200	Running	119,923
	21	Indianapolis — Brickyard 400	10	36	No. 8 Budweiser Chevrolet	160	Running	161,833
	22	Watkins Glen — Global Crossing at The Glen	12	27	No. 8 Budweiser Chevrolet	90	Running	69,788
	23	Michigan — Pepsi 400	12	12	No. 8 Budweiser Chevrolet	162	Running	75,188
	24	Bristol — Sharpie 500	14	24	No. 8 Budweiser Chevrolet	500	Running	85,063
	25	Darlington — Mountain Dew Southern 500	17	18	No. 8 Budweiser Chevrolet	367	Running	74,788
	26	Richmond — Monte Carlo 400	3	8	No. 8 Budweiser Chevrolet	400	Running	106,053
	27	Dover — MBNA Cal Ripken Jr. 400	1	3	No. 8 Budweiser Chevrolet	400	Running	168,858
	28	Kansas — Protection One 400	33	22	No. 8 Budweiser Chevrolet	228	Accident	80,423
	29	Charlotte — UAW-GM Quality 500	4	9	No. 8 Budweiser Chevrolet	334	Running	104,923
	30	Martinsville — Old Dominion 500	27	2	No. 8 Budweiser Chevrolet	496	Running	67,623
	31	Talladega — EA Sports 500	1	6	No. 8 Budweiser Chevrolet	188	Running	165,773
	32	Phoenix — Checker Auto Parts 500	37	30	No. 8 Budweiser Chevrolet	287	Engine	73,248
	33	Rockingham — Pop Secret 400	15	21	No. 8 Budweiser Chevrolet	391	Running	75,223
	34	Homestead — Pennzoil 400	15	17	No. 8 Budweiser Chevrolet	267	Running	77,373

Year	Race No.	Race	Finish	Start	Car	Laps	Condition	Winnings
	35	Atlanta — NAPA 500	7	1	No. 8 Budweiser Chevrolet	325	Running	$122,123
	36	New Hampshire — New Hampshire 300	24	8	No. 8 Budweiser Chevrolet	297	Running	72,948
2000	1	Daytona — Daytona 500	13	8	No. 8 Budweiser Chevrolet	200	Running	107,775
	2	Rockingham — DuraLube/Kmart 400	19	7	No. 8 Budweiser Chevrolet	390	Running	27,110
	3	Las Vegas — carsdirect.com 400	10	3	No. 8 Budweiser Chevrolet	148	Running	76,275
	4	Atlanta — Cracker Barrel 500	29	2	No. 8 Budweiser Chevrolet	307	Running	25,805
	5	Darlington — Mall.com 400	40	10	No. 8 Budweiser Chevrolet	213	Accident	23,375
	6	Bristol — Food City 500	38	12	No. 8 Budweiser Chevrolet	401	Accident	26,235
	7	Texas — DIRECTV 500	1	4	No. 8 Budweiser Chevrolet	334	Running	374,675
	8	Martinsville — Goody's Body Pain 500	26	22	No. 8 Budweiser Chevrolet	496	Running	33,975
	9	Talladega — Die Hard 500	42	6	No. 8 Budweiser Chevrolet	113	Engine	42,850
	10	California — NAPA Auto Parts 500	12	20	No. 8 Budweiser Chevrolet	250	Running	52,375
	11	Richmond — Pontiac Excitement 400	1	5	No. 8 Budweiser Chevrolet	400	Running	118,850
	12	Charlotte — Coca-Cola 600	4	1	No. 8 Budweiser Chevrolet	400	Running	110,900
	13	Dover — MBNA Platinum 400	10	6	No. 8 Budweiser Chevrolet	398	Running	54,785
	14	Michigan — Kmart 400	13	6	No. 8 Budweiser Chevrolet	193	Running	38,200
	15	Pocono — Pocono 500	19	15	No. 8 Budweiser Chevrolet	200	Running	44,015
	16	Sears Point — Save Mart/Kragen 350k	24	31	No. 8 Budweiser Chevrolet	112	Running	47,550
	17	Daytona — Pepsi 400	35	31	No. 8 Budweiser Chevrolet	159	Running	45,330
	18	New Hampshire — thatlook.com 300	21	26	No. 8 Budweiser Chevrolet	272	Running	51,075
	19	Pocono — Pennsylvania 500	13	15	No. 8 Budweiser Chevrolet	200	Running	43,015
	20	Indianapolis — Brickyard 400	13	6	No. 8 Budweiser Chevrolet	160	Running	124,260
	21	Watkins Glen — Global Crossing at The Glen	40	14	No. 8 Budweiser Chevrolet	60	Transmission	34,830
	22	Michigan — Pepsi 400	31	1	No. 8 Budweiser Chevrolet	199	Running	37,730
	23	Bristol — goracing.com 500	21	12	No. 8 Budweiser Chevrolet	499	Running	40,885
	24	Darlington — Pepsi Southern 500	11	13	No. 8 Budweiser Chevrolet	328	Running	46,345
	25	Richmond — Chevrolet Monte Carlo 400	13	31	No. 8 Budweiser Chevrolet	399	Running	37,905
	26	New Hampshire — Dura Lube 300	31	20	No. 8 Budweiser Chevrolet	288	Accident	47,100
	27	Dover — MBNA.com 400	16	13	No. 8 Budweiser Chevrolet	399	Running	55,190
	28	Martinsville — NAPA AutoCare 500	36	32	No. 8 Budweiser Chevrolet	406	Accident	31,500
	29	Charlotte — UAW-GM Quality 500	19	13	No. 8 Budweiser Chevrolet	334	Running	34,390
	30	Talladega — Winston 500	14	3	No. 8 Budweiser Chevrolet	188	Running	49,260
	31	Rockingham — Pop Secret 400	34	37	No. 8 Budweiser Chevrolet	301	Accident	33,550
	32	Phoenix — Checker/DuraLube 500K	27	18	No. 8 Budweiser Chevrolet	311	Running	49,625
	33	Homestead — Pennzoil 400	13	12	No. 8 Budweiser Chevrolet	265	Running	49,525
	34	Atlanta — NAPA 500	20	40	No. 8 Budweiser Chevrolet	322	Running	50,810
1999	12	Charlotte — Coca-Cola 600	16	8	No. 8 Budweiser Chevrolet	397	Running	36,250
	18	New Hampshire — Jiffy Lube 300	43	13	No. 8 Budweiser Chevrolet	44	Ignition	36,475
	22	Michigan — Pepsi 400	24	17	No. 8 Budweiser Chevrolet	199	Running	21,765
	25	Richmond — Exide Select Batteries 400	10	21	No. 8 Budweiser Chevrolet	399	Running	29,905
	34	Atlanta — NAPA 500	14	13	No. 8 Budweiser Chevrolet	324	Running	37,700

BUSCH SERIES (1997–2002)

Year	Race No.	Race	Finish	Start	Car	Laps	Condition	Winnings
2002	1	Daytona – EAS/GNC Live Well 300	1	4	No. 3 Nabisco Oreo Chevrolet	120	Running	$79,175
	13	Charlotte – CARQUEST Auto Parts 300	36	11	No. 3 Nabisco Nilla Chevrolet	83	Accident	10,950
	26	Richmond – Funai 250	1	1	No. 8 Warner Brothers Chevrolet	250	Running	19,850
2001	14	Charlotte – CARQUEST Auto Parts 300	29	33	No. 87 Cellular One Chevrolet	197	Running	9,920
1999	1	Daytona – NAPA Auto Parts 300	14	16	No. 3 ACDelco Chevrolet	120	Running	30,200
	2	Rockingham – ALLTEL 200	35	1	No. 3 ACDelco Chevrolet	126	Accident	15,285
	3	Las Vegas – Sam's Town 300	6	13	No. 3 ACDelco Chevrolet	200	Running	36,400
	4	Atlanta – Yellow Freight 300	3	15	No. 3 ACDelco Chevrolet	195	Running	29,000
	5	Darlington – Diamond Hill Plywood 200	11	5	No. 3 ACDelco Chevrolet	146	Running	17,035
	6	Texas – Coca-Cola 300	10	12	No. 3 ACDelco Chevrolet	163	Running	28,600
	7	Nashville – BellSouth Mobility 320	9	1	No. 3 ACDelco Chevrolet	320	Running	19,235
	8	Bristol – Moore's Snacks 250	2	7	No. 3 ACDelco Chevrolet	250	Running	27,910
	9	Talladega – Touchstone Energy 300	6	17	No. 3 ACDelco Chevrolet	113	Running	27,125
	10	California – Auto Club 300	3	1	No. 3 ACDelco Chevrolet	150	Running	53,875
	11	New Hampshire – New Hampshire 200	34	5	No. 3 ACDelco Chevrolet	193	Accident	17,740
	12	Richmond – Hardee's 250	32	4	No. 3 ACDelco Chevrolet	201	Rear End	15,540
	13	Nazareth – First Union 200	2	3	No. 3 ACDelco Chevrolet	168	Running	26,325
	14	Charlotte – CARQUEST Auto Parts 300	2	22	No. 3 ACDelco Chevrolet	200	Running	45,150
	15	Dover – MBNA Platinum 200	1	15	No. 3 ACDelco Chevrolet	200	Running	44,725
	16	South Boston – Textilease Medique 300	1	1	No. 3 ACDelco Chevrolet	300	Running	36,300
	17	Watkins Glen – Lysol 200	1	3	No. 3 ACDelco Chevrolet	82	Running	37,800
	18	Milwaukee – Die Hard 250	3	15	No. 3 ACDelco Chevrolet	250	Running	27,750
	19	Myrtle Beach – Myrtle Beach 250	25	1	No. 3 ACDelco Chevrolet	247	Running	18,780
	20	Pikes Peak – NAPA AutoCare 250	36	12	No. 3 ACDelco Chevrolet	239	Accident	19,350
	21	Gateway International – CARQUEST Auto Parts 250	1	18	No. 3 ACDelco Chevrolet	200	Running	51,775
	22	Indianapolis Raceway Park – Kroger 200	5	3	No. 3 ACDelco Chevrolet	200	Running	19,125
	23	Michigan – NAPA 200	1	3	No. 3 ACDelco Chevrolet	100	Running	43,650
	24	Bristol – Food City 250	3	5	No. 3 ACDelco Chevrolet	250	Running	25,615
	25	Darlington – Dura Lube 200	12	14	No. 3 ACDelco Chevrolet	146	Running	17,005
	26	Richmond – Autolite Platinum 250	1	20	No. 3 ACDelco Chevrolet	250	Running	35,950
	27	Dover – MBNA.com 200	33	3	No. 3 ACDelco Chevrolet	176	Running	17,300
	28	Charlotte – All Pro Bumper to Bumper 300	5	20	No. 3 ACDelco Chevrolet	200	Running	32,450
	29	Rockingham – Kmart 200	13	2	No. 3 ACDelco Chevrolet	196	Running	17,950
	30	Memphis – Sam's Town 250	2	8	No. 3 ACDelco Chevrolet	250	Running	40,475

Year	Race No.	Race	Finish	Start	Car	Laps	Condition	Winnings
	31	Phoenix – Outback Steakhouse 200	2	5	No. 3 ACDelco Chevrolet	200	Running	$41,075
	32	Homestead – HotWheels.com 300	2	8	No. 3 ACDelco Chevrolet	200	Running	68,700
1998	1	Daytona – NAPA Auto Parts 300	37	3	No. 3 ACDelco Chevrolet	81	Accident	22,925
	2	Rockingham – GM Goodwrench Service Plus 200	16	6	No. 3 ACDelco Chevrolet	197	Running	12,100
	3	Las Vegas – Sam's Town Las Vegas 300	2	8	No. 3 ACDelco Chevrolet	200	Running	59,000
	4	Nashville Speedway USA – BellSouth/Opryland 320	3	7	No. 3 ACDelco Chevrolet	320	Running	24,775
	5	Darlington – Diamond Hill Plywood 200	10	37	No. 3 ACDelco Chevrolet	147	Running	14,425
	6	Bristol – Moore's Snacks 250	2	1	No. 3 ACDelco Chevrolet	250	Running	21,260
	7	Texas – Coca-Cola 300	1	16	No. 3 ACDelco Chevrolet	200	Running	66,075
	8	Hickory – Galaxy Foods 300	8	16	No. 3 ACDelco Chevrolet	300	Running	13,045
	9	Talladega – Touchstone Energy 300	32	4	No. 3 ACDelco Chevrolet	43	Handling	14,300
	10	New Hampshire – Gumout Long Life Formula 200	10	16	No. 3 ACDelco Chevrolet	200	Running	13,475
	11	Nazareth – First Union 200	28	1	No. 3 ACDelco Chevrolet	188	Running	12,925
	12	Charlotte – CARQUEST Auto Parts 300	30	23	No. 3 ACDelco Chevrolet	175	Running	13,245
	13	Dover – MBNA Platinum 200	1	16	No. 3 ACDelco Chevrolet	200	Running	34,075
	14	Richmond – Hardee's 250	2	3	No. 3 ACDelco Chevrolet	250	Running	27,095
	15	Pikes Peak – Lycos.com 250	10	5	No. 3 ACDelco Chevrolet	250	Running	24,000
	16	Watkins Glen – Lysol 200	8	12	No. 3 ACDelco Chevrolet	82	Running	14,150
	17	Milwaukee – Die Hard 250	1	2	No. 3 ACDelco Chevrolet	250	Running	39,625
	18	Myrtle Beach – Myrtle Beach 250	5	3	No. 3 ACDelco Chevrolet	250	Running	17,075
	19	California – Kenwood Home & Car Audio 300	1	2	No. 3 ACDelco Chevrolet	150	Running	68,175
	20	South Boston – Lycos.com 300	13	1	No. 3 ACDelco Chevrolet	299	Running	16,925
	21	Indianapolis Raceway Park – Kroger 200	1	16	No. 3 ACDelco Chevrolet	200	Running	34,225
	22	Michigan – Pepsi 200	5	10	No. 3 ACDelco Chevrolet	100	Running	19,275
	23	Bristol – Food City 250	15	4	No. 3 ACDelco Chevrolet	246	Running	14,490
	24	Darlington – Dura Lube 200	2	34	No. 3 ACDelco Chevrolet	147	Running	28,375
	25	Richmond – Autolite Platinum 250	1	2	No. 3 ACDelco Chevrolet	250	Running	35,600
	26	Dover – MBNA Gold 200	8	17	No. 3 ACDelco Chevrolet	199	Running	16,590
	27	Charlotte – All Pro Bumper to Bumper 300	3	5	No. 3 ACDelco Chevrolet	200	Running	39,325
	28	Gateway International – CARQUEST Auto Parts 250	1	13	No. 3 ACDelco Chevrolet	200	Running	48,525
	29	Rockingham – ACDelco 200	14	8	No. 3 ACDelco Chevrolet	197	Running	15,095
	30	Atlanta – Stihl Outdoor Power Tools 300	2	6	No. 3 ACDelco Chevrolet	195	Running	37,925
	31	Homestead – Jiffy Lube Miami 300	42	15	No. 3 ACDelco Chevrolet	89	Engine	17,470
1997	10	Nashville Speedway USA – BellSouth/Opryland 320	39	19	No. 31 Gargoyles Chevrolet	93	Oil Pump	2,665
	17	Watkins Glen – Lysol 200	39	9	No. 31 Gargoyles Chevrolet	12	Engine	2,525
	20	Gateway International – Gateway 300	38	18	No. 31 Gargoyles Chevrolet	61	Accident	11,400
	22	Michigan – Detroit Gasket 200	7	18	No. 31 Gargoyles Chevrolet	100	Running	6,295
	23	Bristol – Food City 250	22	2	No. 7 Gargoyles Chevrolet	247	Running	4,355
	28	California – Kenwood 300	34	11	No. 31 Gargoyles Chevrolet	129	Handling	11,150
	29	Rockingham – ACDelco 200	16	24	No. 31 ACDelco Chevrolet	197	Running	4,175
	30	Homestead – Jiffy Lube Miami 300	13	14	No. 31 Gargoyles Chevrolet	199	Running	10,315

INDEX

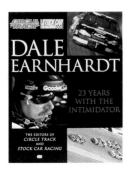

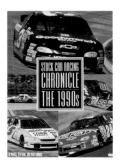
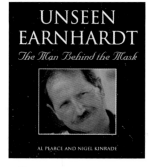
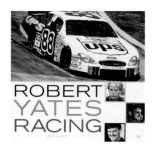

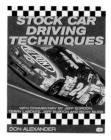